green guide

GARDEN BIRDS

· ·

OF AUSTRALIA

Peter Slater and Sally Elmer

T0001414

First published in 2015 by New Holland Publishers Pty Ltd
Sydney · Auckland

Level 1, 178 Fox Valley Road, Wahroonga, NSW 2076, Australia
5/39 Woodside Avenue, Northcote, Auckland 0627, New Zealand

www.newhollandpublishers.com

ISBN 978 1 92151 750 1

Managing Director: Fiona Schultz
Publisher and Project Editor: Simon Papps
Designer: Thomas Casey
Production Director: Olga Dementiev
Printer: Toppan Leefung Printing Limited

10 9 8 7 6 5 4 3

Front cover images: Red Wattlebird (above left), Galah (left), Scarlet Honeyeater (right),
Barking Owl (below right).
Back cover images: Red-browed Finch (above), Laughing Turtle-Dove (centre),
Torresian Crow (below).
Front flap image: Crested Pigeon.
Page 1: Lewin's Honeyeater
Page 3: Eastern Yellow Robin
Pages 4–5 (main image): Rainbow Lorikeets
Page 5 (inset): Scaly-breasted Lorikeet in grevillea
Pages 20–21 (main image): Scarlet Honeyeater
Page 21 (inset): Pied Butcherbird

Photographic Acknowledgements
All photographs taken by **Peter Slater** and **Sally Elmer** except:
Roger Carter: p11, Spangled Drongo; p13, Red-browed Finches.
Ray Garstone: p24, Brown Quail.
Vera Harper: p89, Spangled Drongo; p93 Red-whiskered Bulbul.
Raoul Slater: p8, Australian Owlet-nightjar chicks; p17, Pale-headed Rosellas at nest box; p70
Satin Bowerbird; p67, Rufous-banded Honeyeater.

Keep up with New Holland Publishers on Facebook
www.facebook.com/NewHollandPublishers

CONTENTS

INTRODUCTION

An Introduction to Australian Birds

❊

When Australia broke away from Antarctica 50 million years ago it became a giant floating ark, carrying with it a host of wild creatures that continued to evolve on the northward journey towards Asia. Among them were birds, descendants from feathered dinosaurs, that adapted to the climatic vicissitudes affecting the island continent: periods of heavy rainfall nurturing dense forests, giant rivers and inland seas; times of prolonged drought; bleak ice ages and inundations from rising water-levels. All influenced the birds, creating new species and condemning others to extinction. The toughest survived and there is now a unique suite of species – birds like lyrebirds, treecreepers, bowerbirds, fairy-wrens, pardalotes, plains-wanderers, megapodes and cockatoos. There have also been imports at various times from the north; birds like herons, ibises, plovers, pipits, larks and swallows that probably initially came as non-breeding migrants but eventually opted to stay. There are still large numbers of migrants; some come to breed, such as kingfishers and cuckoos, others like waders and seabirds arrive after breeding elsewhere. We claim them all as 'Australian'. There are also a number of birds that are not so welcome: they have been deliberately or accidentally introduced into our environment over the past 200 years and compete with native species.

Willie Wagtail.

Crested Pigeon at a ceramic feeder. A pair of Rainbow Lorikeets tried to nest in this feeder.

Australian Garden Birds

Virtually every Australian garden is visited at one time or another by birds. The number and variety of the visitors is determined by the condition and size of the garden. If it is large enough, some birds may reside there permanently. That can be a blessing if the birds are friendly and attractive like doves, robins and honeyeaters, or not quite so welcome in the case of sparrows, brush-turkeys, corellas and Sulphur-crested Cockatoos. Some birds that are friendly throughout most of the year become aggressive while they are breeding, particularly magpies, but also Willie Wagtails if they perceive that their young are threatened. Willie Wagtails can annoy some people by calling loudly on moonlit nights in October and November, while koels also call at night during the summer months. But on the whole, birds are a pleasant adjunct to any garden, particularly those that are planted with birds in mind. Horticulture in Australian gardens is heavily biased towards plants from other countries but thankfully there is a growing enthusiasm for Australian plants like banksias, eucalypts, grevilleas and bottlebrushes that bring birds to the garden. One advantage of many native plants that are attractive to birds is that once established they require little maintenance apart from cutting back periodically. There are large numbers of native plants that are attractive to humans as well as to birds.

What Attracts Birds to Gardens?

Top to bottom: Rainbow Lorikeets; Little Wattlebird; female Superb Fairy-wren.

Food

Birds that regularly visit gardens soon learn to exploit whatever food is on offer. Plants can provide insects, nectar, fruit and seeds, so a well planted garden with multiple food sources will encourage them. Many birds readily accept hand-outs in the form of wild-bird seed mixes, meat, mealworms and nectar mixes, but these may have negative outcomes if used excessively so it is best to ration supplies wisely.

Shelter

Small birds feel most comfortable when there is plenty of thick vegetation to hide in or escape to if danger threatens. A garden with ground cover, some prickly dense shrubbery and a tree or two, will give shelter to a variety of birds. Fairy-wrens, thornbills, scrubwrens and finches will scurry into the lower vegetation; honeyeaters, robins and fantails will hide in the middle reaches; and frogmouths, parrots and pigeons can be found above.

Top to bottom: Little Wattlebirds; Grey Fantail; Eastern Yellow Robin; Australian Owlet-nightjar chicks at entrance of nest box.

Water

Fresh water in bird-baths, ponds or shallow dishes will appeal to any visiting or resident bird, particularly if it is sited next to a bush with suitable perches and enough cover to make the users feel safe from predators. Clean and replenish the water supply daily.

Nest sites

Gardens that are well-stocked with a variety of plants, particularly those that have plenty of prickly foliage, are likely to encourage some birds to build their nests and raise their young. Most likely are robins (centre), thornbills, fairy-wrens, scrubwrens, some honeyeaters, pigeons and butcherbirds. Nest boxes of different sizes, attached to trees at various heights, may be used by parrots, lorikeets and owlet-nightjars (below). There are commercial nest boxes readily available, but they are easy to make by following designs posted on the internet. Hollow logs have been used but they are better left in the bush – each hollow taken from the bush potentially deprives some bird or mammal of a home.

Where is Your Garden?

*C*ity, suburb, rural or coastal? Are you near parkland, lagoons, farming land or native habitat reserves of eucalypt or rainforest? Your local environment will influence what birds are in the area and therefore what you are likely to attract to your garden.

A garden with at least one tree, a number of different flowering and fruiting shrubs, ground-cover and a good layer of leaf-litter or mulch, is the most attractive to birds, and will be appealing to a larger number of species. Each bird species has particular dietary requirements, so it is important to include local plants that will provide a variety of food sources, such as nectar, pollen, fruit, sap, nuts and seeds as well as insects and small lizards. Each food source provides different nutrients, all in balance and essential to happy, healthy birds. They all have their own niche within the habitat – parrots, kookaburras, pigeons and magpies prefer woodland with tall trees including an open canopy so they can observe their surroundings, watching for either predator or prey. Honeyeaters will utilize any plant with nectar-rich flowers, while fairy-wrens and finches like the protection of shrubby vegetation, the fairy-wrens chasing insects and finches searching closer to the ground for grass seed. Scrubwrens, brush-turkeys and magpies scratch around in leaf litter for insects, the magpie also searching over lawns. Then there are the swallows and martins that like open country where they take insects on the wing, as does the aerobatic Grey Fantail, which shoots from a perch to snap at small flying insects.

Courting Crested Pigeons.

Brown Honeyeater.

Planning Your Garden

When planning what to plant and where, take time to consider the design and layout of your garden. If you have space for a tree, where will the shade fall, is it too close to house foundations, drains or overhead powerlines. Is your garden in full sun or shade, does the soil tend to be dry or boggy, sandy or clay. Plants, as well as birds, have particular requirements – some prefer shade, others will only flower in full sun, some don't like wind...

Rainbow Lorikeet feeding in hybrid eucalypt flowers.

When selecting plants, also try to choose species that flower, fruit or seed at different times of year, thus supplying food for the birds year-round. If you have a small garden, it may be best to select a tall bush instead of a tree, to gain the height some birds prefer, but if you have space there are some lovely small trees such as Coral Gum (*Eucalyptus torquata*), mallees or cultivars (above) that have attractive flowers and will not take over the garden. When planning the garden seek the advice of local horticulturalists who can recommend suitably-sized bird-friendly plants.

Mulch
On the ground, a good layer of mulch – around 10cm deep – keeps out weeds and stops the soil getting either too hot or cold and drying out too quickly. As the mulch breaks down, it puts nutrients back into the soil to feed plants and encourages micro-organisms, worms, insects and spiders.

Fertiliser
Australian natives must be fed with a fertiliser specifically for natives. This has to be low in phosphorous as too much will kill them.

Water crystals
Mixing water crystals (which hold a lot of water) with the soil in the bottom of the hole before planting will keep moisture around the roots and reduce the need for watering.

Spangled Drongo.

KEEPING NATIVE SHRUBS BUSHY
Regular pruning of native shrubs after flowering will encourage denser growth.

Native Plants and Their Benefits

Scarlet Honeyeater in Evodia.

*T*here are many Australian natives that will suit the typical suburban garden. Wattles grow all over Australia and come in many sizes and shapes, providing shelter, insects and prolific seed, as well as exudate for birds like the White-eared Honeyeater (below), which licks sap from a Sugar Glider's scrapes. Be aware that some acacias are quite short-lived – less than ten years – but they also have the benefit of improving soil quality. Banksias, callistemons, grevilleas, and hakeas are excellent sources of nectar for honeyeaters, parrots and lorikeets, the nectar also attracting many insects for thornbills and warblers. Melaleucas, closely related to callistemons, are very hardy; the different species, suited to many different environments, come in a range of sizes. Other hardy plants are the leptospermums; their delicate flowers are very attractive to bees and other insects. Lillypillies provide excellent shelter as well as flower and fruit, and have a lush appearance. Closer to ground-level, the unique kangaroo paws, originally from a small corner of Western Australia and now common in many gardens Australia-wide, are enjoyed by small honeyeaters. They complement other low-growing vegetation, including prostrate forms of some of the above plants. Clumps of native grasses like kangaroo grass and wallaby grasses are an important addition as they supply seed for finches and small pigeons.

White-eared Honeyeater licking sap from possum scrape on wattle.

TEA ALTERNATIVE
Leptospermum leaves, were used as a substitute for tea by Captain Cook and his crew, hence the name 'tea tree'.

Native Trees

If you are lucky enough to have acreage, you can reap the benefit of large bird-attracting trees such as majestic eucalypts, silky oak, the beautiful Euodia (left) and even a large shade-giving fig. All of these provide important sources of nectar, manna, fruit and seed.

Importance of Eucalypts

Eucalypts are predominant throughout Australia and have enormous significance to many birds. Their flowers are a major source of food for insects and birds; the fruit and seeds are eaten by parrots and pigeons; and sap is enjoyed by honeyeaters. The leaves are host to many insects, including the bug that creates the lerp (right), a sugary substance that forms a protective shell. Lerps are the staple diet of many small birds such as thornbills and pardalotes, and are enjoyed by many species of honeyeaters. A number of insects excrete honeydew – a sweet liquid licked by honeyeaters – and numerous other insects hide under bark.

Many birds require hollows in which to nest and eucalypts are the most important source of these.

Rufous-throated Honeyeater feeding on Darwin Woollybutt in a tropical garden.

Spotted Pardalote with a bill full of lerps.

ANCIENT GIANTS
A magnificent old eucalypt can provide a multitude of hollows and is a major focal point for a variety of birds.

Spiny-cheeked Honeyeater in Coral Gum.

Water Features: Above Ground or In-ground?

Birds need to drink every day and most also like to bathe, so an important adjunct to the bird-friendly garden is at least one water feature. Birds tend to be very wary while they are drinking or bathing, and with good reason because these are times when they are at their most vulnerable. In the wild predators exploit this dependence by waiting near water-holes. In the garden the main predators are cats, whether a resident or an unwelcome visitor from a neighbour's home, so it is advisable to construct and position the water feature so that cats don't enter the equation. Apart from buying a ready-made bird-bath, you can make one as simply or elaborately as you like and place it close to protective shrubbery. If cats aren't a problem, a pot-plant saucer can be placed on the verandah, on the ground near that shrubbery or hung from a tree. A safer option for the birds is to construct a pedestal using a terracotta pipe, a steel water pipe or a hardwood post with a platform securely fixed on top which accommodates a shallow water-vessel. The

bath should sit about 1.5 metres above the ground. Remember that the water should be replenished daily, and the vessel scrubbed clean to avoid passing on infections like salmonella. If there is a pond in the garden, or a horse-trough in the back paddock, it is good practice to place a convenient perch like a stick or small branch in the water. Some birds like the Crested Pigeon (left) enjoy the sprinkler. Currawongs and butcherbirds occasionally kill small birds, hence the need for sheltering vegetation nearby. Carpet Pythons have been known to wait in this vegetation and take larger birds like pigeons and doves, but they represent a much smaller problem than cats.

Clockwise from top left: Red-browed Finches; Little Wattlebirds; Cattle Egret; Crested Pigeon.

Toads

In the subtropics and tropics toads are a problem in ponds so an eradication regime in the garden makes good sense. To deter toads from breeding, if your pond is at ground-level plant sedges and other dense, low-growing vegetation. If you are planning to build a pond, to keep toads out the outer walls should be 50–60cm high (most frogs can still get in). To prevent water overheating in the sun, the water should be at least one metre deep. To eliminate mosquito larvae from your pond, add some small native fish; some species will also control algae growth. Your local aquarium can advise you. The fish will need shelter from kingfishers and herons, so a rock ledge and some water plants will give them a chance. One heron can clean out all the fish in a pond.

POISON SPAWN
Toad eggs and tadpoles are as toxic as their parents to our wildlife, but some birds, like Cattle Egrets, eat them unharmed.

Dust-bathing

As well as bathing in water, a number of birds like brush-turkeys, Apostlebirds and babblers like to dust-bathe, so a small patch of fine dirt could be left in an isolated corner. A rather bizarre activity allied to feather maintenance or perhaps to discourage feather-mites is 'anting', which involves rubbing ants through the feathers.

Nesting

Eastern Yellow Robin.

*M*ost garden birds use a variety of materials, including sticks, bark, grass, plant-down (from thistle and dandelion) and spiders' webs to build their nests – magpies have stick-nests in the tops of trees; frogmouths, pigeons and doves make flimsy platforms of sticks and the smaller birds mainly use grass, cobwebs and down to construct their cupped, domed or bottle-shaped nests. The Mistletoebird builds almost entirely with cobweb and down, and the Willie Wagtail's very neat nest is tightly held together with web. Magpie-larks and swallows use mud, the former on a branch and the latter under the eaves of houses. Cuckoos don't build but rely on other birds to raise their young. Kookaburras, boobooks, owlet-nightjars, Dollarbirds, cockatoos and parrots rely on tree hollows, and unfortunately have to compete for a diminishing resource as these hollows disappear with deforestation.

Hundred-year-old tree hollows

Hollows are found in aged trees, usually eucalypts over 100 years old, as it takes time for them to develop, either by termites eating away the dead central areas of wood, or through decay where a branch has fallen off leaving the wound open to fungal attack. These old trees can have many hollows of varying sizes to suit different birds (and other fauna), equivalent to multi-storey residential units. This hollow (right), used for many years by Sulphur-crested Cockatoos, was left in a suburban development. Regrettably, many of these remarkable old specimens are destroyed to make way for suburbia or farmland, or if in parkland, because they are considered unsightly or unsafe. To compensate, nest boxes of various sizes and shapes can be placed in trees in the garden or even against the house or shed wall.

Sulphur-crested Cockatoo in tree hollow.

Nest Boxes

*I*n your garden, the birds most likely to use nest boxes are kookaburras, cockatoos, parrots, boobooks, owlet-nightjars and maybe even pardalotes or kestrels. The boxes are easy to make but there are a few points which must be observed; it must be strong and stable, have good insulation and be weatherproof.

Pale-headed Rosellas feeding chick in backyard nest box.

Wood, at least 20mm thick, is a good insulator and the easiest material to use. Metals can get too hot or cold and this can kill chicks which are too young to escape. Hardwood is preferable as it will last longer and does not contain harmful chemicals, unlike chipboard, MDF board, plywood or treated pine. Use galvanised screws or nails to prevent them rusting away and try to close all gaps to exclude drafts and sunlight. Painting the exterior of the box will increase its life, but be sure to use non-toxic external water-based acrylic, and do not paint the entrance hole or interior walls. Oiling is another option. Box lids need to have a slope and preferably an overhang on three sides to shed rainwater, and it is a good idea to drill a few small holes into the bottom of the box to drain any water that may get in. The lid should also be hinged to allow for cleaning after breeding, or to remove pests. To increase ventilation, drill some small holes (3mm in diameter) at the top of the side-walls under the overhang. The interior wall below the entrance hole should be rough so that birds can climb out – to texture the surface, saw 2mm grooves, tack on some shade cloth, fine mesh [no sharp edges] or strips of wood as steps.

Once constructed, the box should be securely fixed to the main trunk of a mature tree, remembering that as the tree grows its diameter will increase, so a wire wrapped around the trunk will gradually strangle and kill the tree. For the best chance of success use a tree with good shade and place the box at least 3 metres off the ground and facing away from the worst of the sun, wind or rain.

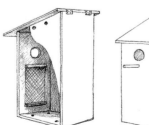

PLEASE!
Do not remove hollows from the bush, as you are depriving other wildlife of their home: nest, shelter or roost. There are many sites on the web with instructions on building boxes for specific birds.

To Feed or Not to Feed?

So many people get so much enjoyment from feeding the birds in their gardens that no amount of argument against the practice will have any effect. Concerned birdwatchers and birdwatching societies suggest that feeding birds is detrimental to their well-being for these reasons: feeding can create dependence on an unnatural food-source; it can lead to over-population with deleterious consequences in the breeding season; it can encourage aggressive species like miners and currawongs, with the effect that more timid species are displaced; it

can encourage introduced feral species like sparrows, Common Blackbirds and Common Mynas, as well as misplaced native birds like corellas and lorikeets outside their natural ranges; it can lead to the spread of pathogens like Beak and Feather Disease if feeding and drinking vessels are not adequately cleaned; and, most seriously, it can directly effect the development of young birds being fed in the nest by their parents with inappropriate hand-outs from well-meaning citizens.

Opposite above: Juvenile Pied Butcherbird; Opposite below: Magpie-lark with mealworms; Above: Australian King-Parrots.

Despite these arguments, birds are still going to be fed in backyards, so some common-sense measures will offset many of the problems just discussed. The first solution is to feed them a more balanced diet. In the wild, meat-eaters consume the whole prey – bones, fur, feathers and viscera – as well as the meat; nectar-feeders also eat insects, pollen and some fruit; and seed-eaters would include fresh green seed and some other vegetation, as well as dried seed which has fallen on the ground. Some of the larger pet supply stores have supplementary mixes that provide necessary vitamins and minerals, essential fatty acids, proteins, meat meal, bone meal, and so on.

For meat-eaters, mix some insectivore powder with the meat. A nectar powder can be mixed with water for honeyeaters and lorikeets. Some fresh fruit and vegetables (such as broccoli) will entice some species. Live mealworms (supplying protein) are relished by many birds, but limit the quantity as they are high in fat and low in calcium. Try to put out seed and other food late in the day so that the birds will have spent the majority of their time gleaning natural sustenance, and the hand-out is just a top-up before bedtime. Limit the amount of food provided – this can be judged by checking if any food is left. If any has not been consumed then too much has been provided and the amount needs to be cut down (excess seed may attract rats and mice). Strictly ration any meat and use only strips of beef heart or specialised substitutes; cease feeding meat at the onset of the breeding season, probably July/August for magpies and a bit later for kookaburras and butcherbirds. It is preferable not to feed meat, seed or nectar to birds that are raising chicks for fear of causing bone and feather deformities. Finally, coordinate feeding regimes with others in the vicinity.

SCRUFFY COCKATOOS
One often sees cockatoos with featherless patches and over-long beaks coming to the feeding table. They are suffering from Beak and Feather Disease, a fatal condition that has no cure. Unfortunately it is transmissible to other birds, so it is essential to clean feeding and drinking vessels thoroughly if such birds turn up.

BIRDS THAT VISIT
AUSTRALIAN GARDENS

Australian Wood Duck

Over the past 50 years the grass-feeding wood duck has steadily increased in numbers around most wetlands, from lakes to dams, as well as pastures in the country and lawns and street verges in towns and city suburbs. It is now a common sight to see a pair of wood ducks shepherding their brood of up to a dozen ducklings across a roadway, and some shire councils have erected signs advising motorists to take care. The favourite nest-site is a large hollow branch usually at some height in a tree. Between seven and fourteen eggs hatch into chicks that are at first downy but soon grow a plumage similar to the female's but more attractively streaked.

DARE-DEVIL CHICKS
Once hatched, the down-clad wood duck chicks jump from their nest hollow to the ground, usually alighting without damage even from a height of 10–20 metres.

Straw-necked Ibis

Although not as abundant as the white ibis, Straw-necks are nevertheless common, but not to the extent of being considered a pest. On the contrary, their appetite for insects such as grasshoppers in farmlands and lawn grubs in urban settings should make them welcome visitors. They sometimes occur in large flocks and breed

colonially, often together with white ibis and other waterbirds, usually in lignum and paperbark swamps. Two to four chicks are raised in a stick-nest. Like the other birds on these two pages, ibises are unlikely to occur in small gardens, mainly because of difficulty of access, but larger gardens with expanses of lawn are quite likely to inspire a visit.

Australian White Ibis

Another bird that has increased in numbers, though more dramatically than the wood duck, the white ibis has reached pest status in some urban parks and gardens, despite efforts to discourage the public from feeding them. They are often seen in large numbers scavenging in public refuse-tips. A recently moulted bird like this one is quite handsome but in urban situations the feathers soon become grubby and soiled. Any expanse of lawn will encourage them to probe for insects like crickets and grubs, so the occasional visit is of benefit to the garden. The long curved beak is very sensitive and can detect insects in the soil. They nest in trees and palms in colonies, usually near or over water, even in towns, laying two to four eggs in a stick-nest. This species is very similar to the Sacred Ibis of sub-Saharan Africa.

White-faced Heron

This heron, feeding as often on dry land as it does in wetlands, is an occasional visitor to large gardens, where it searches for insects in lawns and garden-beds as well as fish and tadpoles in unprotected ponds. It is interesting to watch how they flush their prey, pattering the ground with one foot and waggling the neck from side to side while the head remains motionless, hoping to surprise grasshoppers and other invertebrates. Their long 'S'-shaped neck can be folded down while resting, making them appear neck-less. They are generally solitary, and build flat untidy stick-nests in isolated trees, often far from water. Three to five light blue-green eggs complete the clutch.

Australian Brush-turkey

While they have a fascinating life-story, brush-turkeys are not always appreciated in gardens when they appear. To make its nest-mound the male spends much of its time scratching up debris including leaves, sticks, mulch and, regrettably, more than the occasional garden plant. They are so single-minded that they will continue to scratch over barriers, paths and even across roads in the effort to provide a repository for the eggs which any visiting females choose to lay. Breeding males develop pendulous wattles. The internal temperature of the mound is kept warm by the decomposition of plant debris. Once the eggs are laid the male regulates the temperature by removing or adding to the top layers. Eight to fifteen eggs may be laid in a mound over a period of several months. After an incubation period of about 50 days the eggs hatch and chicks, with fully developed flight feathers, dig their way out of the mound and head for cover to make their own way in the world.

> **HEAT DETERMINES SEX**
> Internal mound temperature determines the sex of brush-turkey chicks. At 34°C there are an equal ratio of males to females – higher temperatures result in more females, lower temperatures create more males.

Brown Quail

One would not expect quail to visit gardens, but given the right conditions of long grass, particularly adjacent to bush-land, Brown Quail, like this bird, could turn up to glean seeds fallen from the feeding table. They tend to keep well hidden in tangled vegetation, but reveal their presence with a loud ascending double whistle, 'wh-wheer'. While feeding they adopt a horizontal position, but if startled run with neck stretched up like a giraffe. When pressed they take to the air with a loud whirr, alighting at some distance into long grass. The nest is well hidden in grass and contains four to seven spotted eggs. When hatched the young birds follow the hen like tiny barnyard chickens.

Southern Stone-curlew

Despite its name this nocturnal ground-bird is found in northern Australia as well as the south. It has largely disappeared from Victoria but still persists elsewhere, despite vulnerability to predation from dogs, cats and foxes during the breeding season. In Brisbane it is common in parks, vacant allotments and large gardens, and its loud wailing calls are often heard at night. This bird, shown changing over incubation duties just after sun-down at a nest in a suburban lot, laid three times in one season but failed on each occasion due to heavy rain.

Masked Lapwing

Lapwings are large plovers with loud calls and they aggressively defend their young when breeding. Many species have wattled faces to protect feathers when digging in soft ground for food, but none as pronounced as the Masked, particularly in birds in northern Australia. Birds in the east have a black semi-collar, which is lacking in northern birds. A sparse nest is made on the ground and four mottled eggs are laid. In towns and suburbs any expanse of lawn or short grass can be chosen as a nest-site. Once the chicks hatch the parents defend the nest vigorously against intruders including dogs, cats, horses and humans.

ARMED FOR COMBAT
Plovers have a spur on each wing to aid in nest defence.

Predatory Birds

Some birds that visit gardens are generally regarded as birds of prey, which is something of a misnomer as the majority of birds prey on other living creatures, mainly invertebrates like mosquitoes, scorpions, worms, grubs and grasshoppers. Many predatory birds that feed on warm-blooded creatures are not usually thought of as birds of prey; they include kookaburras, butcherbirds, magpies and currawongs as well as occasional predators like shrike-thrushes and drongos. But those thought of as birds of prey, or raptors, include warm-blooded creatures in their diets, and over the passage of time have developed physical attributes as well as strategies that enable them to capture their victims. Most have strong claws and hooked beaks to help tear up their quarry into bite-sized pieces. Falcons are capable of swift flight, sparrowhawks utilise rapid manoeuvres on broad wings in following their victims' desperate attempts to evade capture, owls have soft edges to their flight feathers to

> **MUM'S THE BOSS**
> With Australian raptors, the female is much larger than the male

aid silent flight and specialised ears to help detect their quarry at night, frogmouths have wide gapes to capture their prey. As hunters, a raptor's eyesight is very sharp – two to eight times better than humans – thus the term 'hawk-eyed'. The hovering kestrel spots grasshoppers and lizards from a height of up to 40 metres.

Collared Sparrowhawk

An intelligent raptor, the sparrowhawk probably knows all the gardens within its large territory where kindly souls regularly feed finches, doves, pigeons and other birds. Its hunting success depends on secretive behaviour so it usually makes its attacks on these birds without being noticed by the providers of largesse. It is most likely to occur in outer urban gardens close to woodlands that provide sanctuary and nest-sites. Pairs differ in size, the females being much larger than the male, so they sample a wide range of prey, from small finches to pigeons. They are very territorial so an entire suburb or small town might be covered by only a few pairs. The similar but larger Brown Goshawk is less common in urban environments.

Nankeen Kestrel

Kestrels are small falcons that feed principally on mice, lizards and grasshoppers that they detect while hovering in the air. Nankeen is the colour of a cloth popular in the 19th century. In urban environments they seek prey in vacant lots, and often choose cavities in buildings to house their four or five beautifully marked eggs. Normally kestrels nest in hollow limbs of large trees, but they will also do so in caves and natural holes in rocky cliffs, and as far as they are concerned, buildings are just an extension of their world. No nest is constructed; eggs are incubated for about 28 days and the chicks remain in the cavity for a similar period.

Pacific Baza

Any eastern or northern garden with large trees that harbour tree-frogs and phasmids, from about Sydney to Broome, is likely to be visited by bazas. Outside the breeding season they move in small flocks, and may stay in a garden for a few days while they glean the leaves for their favoured prey. With large staring eyes they can detect camouflaged victims with ease, then swoop and cling onto the leaves, often upside down, while the victim is seized and carried to a nearby perch. As the breeding season approaches they pair up and perform back-peddling aerial displays, rather like the way they take their prey, accompanied by a loud 'ee-chew'. Their stick-nests are placed in tall trees.

Southern Boobook

The boobook is found all over Australia
and Tasmania, wherever there are trees
with hollows to nest in. Gardens that
abut woodlands and are well planted
with trees are the most likely to attract
these small owls. They are quite vocal
at night, particularly in the breeding
season, and their disyllabic call,
rendered variously as 'mo-poke', 'book-
book', 'more-pork' or 'wook-wook', has
assumed iconic status. During the day
they rest well-hidden on a favourite
leafy branch. This bird, for instance,
used the same day-time perch for many
months without being harassed. If not
hidden well enough, boobooks will be
mobbed by other birds, particularly
magpies, drongos and miners.

Australian Owlet-nightjar

This delightful little night bird is found
all over Australia. It occurs in two
colour morphs: reddish in drier areas
and grey in more humid environments.
During the day it rests in a hollow
tree-limb, either horizontal or vertical,
and may often be seen at the entrance
enjoying the sun. If disturbed it pops
back inside but, being curious, emerges
after a minute or two to check its
surroundings. It has a far-carrying
chuckling call, uttered during the day
as well as at night. It feeds mainly on
flying insects like moths and often
sits on the ground so it can see its
prey silhouetted above, flying up like
a nocturnal Willie Wagtail. In outer
suburban and country gardens it will
use nest boxes.

Tawny Frogmouth

A common garden bird throughout Australia, the frogmouth also has a number of colour variants. Females generally are rather more reddish on the shoulders than males, but in the deserts, in the north and occasionally elsewhere, females can be a very attractive bright rufous all over. During the day frogmouths sit on a tree-branch, usually close to the main trunk, and if disturbed assume an elongated posture mimicking a dead stick. On a cold morning they will often fly down to the ground and soak up the sun's rays with outstretched wings. In warmer months they accumulate body fat, and they rely on this during colder months when their food, principally insects, is not so readily available. In past decades pesticides accumulated in the body fat and when cold weather arrived these were apparently released into the body resulting in paralysis. Affected birds were often picked up in gardens. Thankfully these chemicals are no longer in use and such paralysed birds seem to be a thing of the past. However it is a reminder of the hazards of using chemicals in the garden. Frogmouths often return to the same nest-site each year and build a flimsy nest from twigs on a horizontal branch. They usually lay two white eggs but clutches of one and three are occasionally reported. Males incubate during the day, females at night.

> **WHICH IS THE TRUE MOPOKE?**
> The familiar 'mopoke' call heard at night is believed by many to be uttered by the Tawny Frogmouth, but in reality the call emanates from the Southern Boobook owl. The frogmouth's call is a quiet repetitive 'oom-oom-oom'.

Seeing at Night?

*O*wls have a number of adaptations that enable them to see effectively at night, although their ability to perceive colour is limited. The eyes occupy a large proportion of the skull and are directed forward to facilitate stereoscopic vision; most of the receptors at the back of

Above: Barking Owl; Below: Pheasant Coucal.

the eye are light-sensitive rods (most of ours are colour-sensitive cones); behind the layer of rods is a mirror-like layer that reflects incoming light back to the rods, virtually doubling the amount of light activating them. The shape of the eye is more elliptical than ours and the cornea is larger also, allowing more light to reach the rods. During the day, the pupil closes right down to protect the light-sensitive rods from overload. Due to the size of the eyes, owls are not able to swivel them and can only see directly forward, so they have to turn the head instead. Frogmouths and owlet-nightjars are similarly adapted for nocturnal vision.

> **SEEING WITH EARS**
> As well as sight, owls also rely heavily on hearing; they have large ear openings with one positioned higher than the other. These features allow them to find their prey with remarkable accuracy, even in total darkness.

Dinosaurs in the Garden?

*S*ome warm-blooded dinosaurs developed a covering of hair-like down that aided them in regulating their body-heat. Over time the down evolved into feathers that were so successful in keeping an even temperature that these small dinosaurs were able to withstand the events that exterminated their larger relatives. The feathers on the fore-limbs and tail became more elongated, eventually leading to the ability to glide, then to fly. The bones of the fore-limbs lost fingers and the tail-bones shortened and disappeared; the skull lost teeth and the snout grew into a beak. They possibly looked rather like the Pheasant Coucal (right). At no point in time did the dinosaur end and the bird begin – what we know now as birds are in reality dinosaurs in modern guise. After the catastrophic events that exterminated most dinosaurs and many other animal

groups as well, there were numerous vacant gaps in the environment that the survivors could exploit. The ability to fly enabled bird/dinosaurs to expand successfully into these niches in three dimensions. The basic design of the original 'bird' evolved into the various forms that share our world. Are there dinosaurs in the garden? The answer is 'yes'.

Preening

*I*t can be entertaining watching birds preen; they have thousands of feathers to maintain which leads to some very interesting postures. Healthy feathers are essential and most birds preen several times a day. With beak and toes they remove dirt, parasites and mites, and any tough sheaths from newly moulted feathers, then rearrange any out-of-place feathers. Most birds have a preen gland at the base of their tail which excretes a

Rainbow Lorikeet maintaining its tail-feathers.

special oil that is spread over the feathers to keep them healthy, shiny and flexible. Some birds – owls, parrots, pigeons and herons – don't have this preen gland, but have powder-down feathers which grow continuously and gradually disintegrate into a fine powder down which filters through their feathers. These feathers then need to be properly aligned for insulation, waterproofing and streamlining for flight. Allo-preening, or mutual preening, strengthens bonds between mates.

Associated with preening are bathing in either water or dust, stretching, anting (see page 15) and sunning. Birds sunbathe by ruffling up their feathers and spreading out tail and wings to expose skin and feathers to the sun. When approaching what appears to be a dead or sick bird, it can be quite startling when they suddenly come to life. While sunning, birds can become too relaxed and less wary, making them easy prey for cats!

> ### SWIVELLING NECKS
> Birds have more neck (cervical) vertebrae than we do – from 13 to 25 – which allows great flexibility. We have 7. Owls with 14 can turn their heads 270°. Parrots have 10.

Coping with Indigestible Material

*B*irds such as owls, raptors, kookaburras, butcherbirds and magpies are unable to digest fur, bones, feathers, invertebrate exo-skeletons and hard seeds. These items accumulate in the crop and are compressed into a pellet, which is coughed up. Examination of the pellets gives some idea of what is being eaten. Birds like currawongs often regurgitate their pellets into water features in the garden.

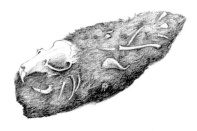

Doves and Pigeons

*B*asically there is no anatomical difference between doves and pigeons – in general doves are small and pigeons are large, but there is so much overlap in size that the distinctions are arbitrary. They feed on either fruit or seeds. Most of the species that visit gardens are graminivorous, attracted by seeds provided by householders. Many commercial seed mixes include a variety of seed sizes, catering for the preferences of different species, so usually more than one will regularly visit. They benefit more from native grasses planted in the garden as they have to actively move about to find seeds, both green and ripe. The most common visitor is the Crested Pigeon, which quickly becomes tame and if the garden is big enough may take up residence, the male entertaining gardeners as he flirts with and chases the females. Others like the Common Bronzewing tend to be more reticent. Unlike most other birds, pigeons drink very quickly by sucking up water. Pigeons and doves make flimsy stick-nests and lay one or two white eggs. Chicks are fed by the parents with regurgitated 'pigeon's milk' and partly digested seeds or fruit.

The Spotted Turtle-Dove is an introduced species, originally from south Asia. In Australia it is virtually confined to the vicinity of human habitation in the south-west of Western Australia and in the east from Port Lincoln, South Australia, to Cooktown, Queensland.

The Peaceful Dove is found over most of Australia except southern Western Australia, even in deserts if water is available. It readily adapts to human habitation, like this bird nesting in a suburban garden. It has benefited from our environmental impact.

The Bar-shouldered Dove inhabits north-western, northern and eastern Australia, from about Exmouth, Western Australia, to north-eastern Victoria. This individual is sunbathing in typical pigeon fashion.

The dainty little Diamond Dove is common over the northern four-fifths of Australia, but it is virtually absent from the southern fringe. It is common in drier areas and appreciates the provision of water.

The down feathers of pigeons and doves, particularly on the flanks, provide a fine powder which is spread over the outer feathers while preening. If a bird is startled in the garden and flies into a closed window, the powder-down leaves an imprint of the impact on the glass. If a bird hits the glass at the right angle a perfect impression of the wings and body is left. Occasionally the sudden appearance of a sparrowhawk will cause a bird to hit a window, leaving it momentarily stunned, and thus easy prey.

The Laughing Turtle-Dove is another introduced species, originally from Africa or India. It is common in urban areas in the south-west of Western Australia. To some ears its call resembles a giggling laugh, hence the name.

WHAT IS PIGEON'S MILK?
For the first few days after hatching, the chicks of pigeons and doves are fed with secretions from the lining of the crops of their parents. This nutrient-rich liquid is known as 'crop-milk' or 'pigeon's milk'.

Crested Pigeon

One of the commonest pigeons throughout Australia, the Crested has proliferated in the wake of our changes to the environment, finding land clearing, provision of water and seeding pasture plants to its liking. In cities and towns it does well, and is one of the first birds to exploit handouts in the form of seed and water in gardens. The iridescent feathers in the wings are seen to best advantage when males, seeking an available female, perform their bowing courtship displays. They build a flat nest made up of twigs, usually well-hidden in dense vegetation, either in a bush or a tree. Two white eggs are laid, which may be abandoned if disturbed.

WHISTLE WINGS

In flight, the wings of the Crested Pigeon make a whistling sound due to the narrowing of the third primary feather. Some doves have a narrow outer primary.

Common Bronzewing

This bronzewing is just as widespread as the Crested Pigeon, but is not as common, despite its name. However, its range does extend into Tasmania, where the Crested does not occur. The iridescent wing-feathers are even more spectacular in displays than those of the Crested. The female is not as colourful as the male and lacks the lovely apricot colouring on the forehead. She does most of the building of a flimsy

stick-nest which is placed at no great height in a tree. She performs most of the incubation duties and sits very tightly, but if flushed inadvertently from her eggs she is likely to abandon them and rebuild elsewhere. If the pair finds a favoured nest site which is not disturbed they may reuse it for several seasons. So, if they nest in the garden, approach with caution.

White-headed Pigeon

This is a young White-headed Pigeon; adults are more attractively plumaged with iridescent fringes to the back-feathers and unusual crimping on the neck-feathers. Although related to the Rock Dove, they are more like rainforest fruit-doves in behaviour, but unlike them will also descend to the ground to feed on fallen fruit. They are partial to the introduced Camphor Laurel and are partly responsible for its spread. In outer suburbs adjacent to forests along the eastern fringe of Australia they readily accept seed handouts.

Feral Pigeon

The pigeons that abound in and around cities and towns are derived from the numerous varieties of the domestic pigeon, which in turn were developed over the past several thousand years from the Rock Dove. Their swift flight and homing ability made them ideal message carriers in the past, and are still used in pigeon racing. Nowadays the natural populations of the Rock Dove are struggling to maintain genetic purity in the face of the spread of feral pigeons. There are no pure Rock Doves in Australia, but feral flocks abound, augmented by escapees from pigeon lofts. In general any of the more showy varieties that join the feral flocks are quickly weeded out by birds of prey so most of the birds that survive are similar in appearance to the original Rock Dove. Given time they will probably revert to the wild type, that is, grey with two dark bars on the wing. A stick-nest is built in a tree-cavity, on rock-faces or in niches in buildings (pigeon holes!). Two white eggs are laid.

FINDING A WAY HOME?
Homing pigeons have been selectively bred to return home over long distances. Theories as to how they achieve this include the use of the earth's magnetic field lines, odour, orientation from the sun and infrasound.

Cockatoos, Lorikeets and Parrots

*T*hese birds are among the most frequent visitors to gardens, and in fact some will take over the feeding-table to the detriment of other species. There is something of a pecking-order; Rainbow Lorikeets tend to bluff even much bigger birds like pigeons, cockatoos and brush-turkeys. In our yard there is a stalemate, though, between the Rainbows and Apostlebirds. However, if wild-bird seed-mixes

> ### PIGEON-TOED PARROTS
> Parrots have two toes on each foot directed forward and two directed backward, enabling them to grasp seeds and fruit while their strong curved beaks break off manageable portions. When they walk their gait is more pigeon-toed than pigeons.

are provided, different species with different seed-preferences will feed together relatively amicably, and lorikeets, cockatoos and parrots provide a kaleidoscope of colour. All of the species likely to be seen in gardens nest in hollows in trees, often competing for ever diminishing sites with feral bees, possums, starlings and owls. In the garden this can be compensated for with appropriate nest boxes, but they tend to be taken over by Rainbow Lorikeets. All species lay white eggs.

Galah

Perhaps familiarity obscures our appreciation of what is a truly spectacular bird, particularly when observed wheeling, alternately pink and grey, in large, sometimes huge, flocks. Galahs are one of the species that has benefited from our changes to the environment, and are now among the most commonly sighted birds throughout Australia, wherever there is available water. In urban areas and country towns they commonly feed along road-verges and in parks, and in gardens as well. They tend to be rather destructive of eucalypts, snipping off leafy twigs, some of which are carried to nesting hollows, possibly to deter insect infestations. Usually three or four white eggs are laid. Very occasionally in garden situations Galahs will hybridise with other species of cockatoo. A hybrid Galah x Little Corella that visited our yard was a beautiful apricot colour.

Sulphur-crested Cockatoo

Outside the breeding season these cockatoos gather in flocks. Once they find a garden feeding station they will regularly descend in increasing numbers as the word gets out. While in the garden they will also feed on other things as well, from weeds in the lawn to seed-pods of Cape Tulips and Tipuana, to say nothing of ripening fruit like peaches and mandarins and nuts like macadamia. One often sees individuals afflicted with Beak and Feather Disease and with overgrown beaks that make feeding difficult, basically only kept alive by the seed handouts. This surprisingly large and raucous bird can be very destructive around the home.

Gang-gang Cockatoo

The Gang-gang, quiet and unobtrusive, is common in Canberra, visiting gardens with hawthorn hedges, seeking the berries. It is quite tame while feeding. Elsewhere in the south-east it is not so common, but occasionally occurs in large flocks of up to 50 birds in and near forests in winter.

Little Corella

The Little Corella is basically a bird of the inland and is common in many country towns. In coastal city suburbs they occur in noisy flocks, many of which appear to be descended from aviary escapees. Likewise the similar Long-billed Corella has a presence in suburbs well away from its normal range in the south-east. Both visit feeding-tables.

Australian King-Parrot

An early colonial account referred to this bird as 'Governor King's Parrot'; apparently his dress uniform was scarlet and green. It is a regular visitor to feeding-tables in eastern gardens, often arriving in small flocks including females and young birds that lack the scarlet colouring and are basically green all over. At about one year old males begin acquiring adult dress and for a while wear scattered red feathers amidst the green. King- Parrots may attack bananas growing in the garden while still unripe. Three to five white eggs are laid in a deep vertical tree-hollow. The female incubates the eggs and is fed at the nest by the male. Once the chicks hatch both parents feed them. The young are soon independent but generally stay with the parents, often joining other family groups until the following breeding season.

Australian Ringneck

Common in drier woodlands, the ringneck is variable in plumage across Australia. In the west and centre the head is black (lower right: in a garden in Alice Springs); in the east the head is a mixture of red, green and blue (below left: in a garden in Tambo, Queensland); in north-west Queensland the head is green and this form is commonly called the Cloncurry Parrot. All colour varieties share the yellow collar that gives the bird its name.

Black-Cockatoos

Banksias, hakeas and pines in very large gardens are likely to attract occasional small flocks of Black-Cockatoos – Yellow-tailed in the east and Tasmania and Carnaby's in the south-west. Other species like the Red-tailed, Glossy and Baudin's are not likely to occur in gardens although we did see a flock of Red-tailed feeding on the ground in an outback Queensland backyard. They can

be destructive of foliage; we noticed a car in Perth, parked under a pine tree, literally covered in branchlets snipped off by the Carnaby's Black-Cockatoos while feeding on the cones. They nest in large hollows and lay one or two white eggs. The chicks are dependent on their parents for a long time so pairs do not necessarily breed every year. Young ones are very noisy as they follow the adults, begging for food.

Red-rumped Parrot

Often seen feeding along roadsides, the Red-rumped Parrot is a common woodland bird in south-eastern Australia, from about Port Augusta, South Australia, to southern Queensland, although its range doesn't extend into Tasmania. It feeds mainly on the ground, and those we have watched seem to prefer fossicking for seeds in the shade, running quickly from patch to patch of suitable shaded herbage. Early in the morning pairs will perch together on exposed twigs soaking up the first rays of sunlight. For much of the year they feed in loose flocks, but as the breeding season approaches they become more territorial and often dispute nest-sites. Four to six white eggs are laid in an unlined eucalypt hollow; they will use nest boxes.

FEEDING CHICKS
To feed their chicks parrots first swallow and partly digest seeds then regurgitate them into the beaks of their youngsters.

Rainbow Lorikeet

Any garden in the east and north that features grevilleas, callistemons and eucalypts is likely to attract lorikeets. They will visit the feeding table for seeds as well and don't mind the occasional nibble at ripening fruit in the garden. They are quite bossy and confront other species while they are feeding. In northern Australia, from about Broome, Western Australia, to Karumba, Queensland, there occurs a brightly coloured race, the Red-collared Lorikeet (centre left). In Perth, Western Australia, and surrounds, there are large flocks of feral lorikeets which have descended from aviary escapees. In the east and north they will use nest boxes in the garden.

Scaly-breasted Lorikeet

Ranging in the east from about Cooktown, Queensland, to Sydney, New South Wales, and sporadically further south, the Scaly-breasted Lorikeet also occurs as a feral population around Melbourne, Victoria. Its range appears to be expanding, particularly on Cape York Peninsula. Flight is swift and reveals the red and yellow underwing. It commonly visits feeding tables and flowering plants in gardens, and will utilise nest boxes. Elsewhere it nests in tree-hollows and knot-holes and usually lays two white eggs.

> **HOW DO LORIKEETS FEED?**
> Lorikeets take nectar and pollen from flowers with a specially adapted brush tongue. Efficient feeders, they can take sustenance from up to 30 flowers per minute, and need to visit as many as 5,000 flowers per day.

Musk Lorikeet

In 1865 John Gould wrote that the Tasmanian colonists called this bird the 'Musk-Parrakeet' from the "peculiar odour it emits". It is confined to Tasmania and the south-east from Eyre Peninsula, South Australia, to Nanango, south-eastern Queensland. It regularly visits flowers in gardens, preferring eucalypts, and has increased in numbers in Adelaide and Melbourne. Unfortunately, in fruit-growing areas it is something of a pest, but in the garden is an attractive, active visitor. It nests in eucalypt tree-hollows and usually lays two white eggs.

Small lorikeets

The red-faced Little Lorikeet (upper) usually feeds high in flowering eucalypts and in clumps of mistletoe. It commonly visits eucalypts in our garden but has never been seen at the feeding-table, nor in our grevilleas. It occurs in the east from Yorke Peninsula, South Australia, to Cairns, Queensland. The range of the similar but more attractive Purple-crowned Lorikeet (lower) extends from Victoria to Western Australia.

Varied Lorikeet

A tropical species, the range of the beautiful Varied Lorikeet extends from Bamaga, Queensland, to Broome, Western Australia. When the bloodwood eucalypts are flowering, usually from July–September, it may be found further south in the Channel Country. It is relatively quiet while feeding and usually flies in small flocks, but occasionally in larger groups; there is one record of 'thousands'. It nests in the drier winter months in a eucalypt hollow or knot-hole and lays three to five eggs.

Rosellas

*M*edium-sized broad-tailed parrots, the rosellas respond well to seed and water provided for them in gardens. Their main habitats are forests and woodlands from Tasmania and South Australia northward to Cape York, northern Australia and also in the south-west. They are usually seen in pairs or small flocks, feeding on the seeds of wattle, gum-nuts, grasses, thistles, clover and fruit. When chatting to each other in the trees, they will often give a sideways waggle of the tail. In most cases males and females are similar in plumage but the female Western Rosella is more green, the red colouring confined to the forehead and scattered feathers on the breast and abdomen. Young birds are generally duller in colouration. In the south-east young Crimson Rosellas are basically green with red patches, but in the north, youngsters are much like the adult. Identification can become confusing where the ranges of some species meet and interbreeding results in mixed colours. Nesting is in hollow tree-limbs and nest boxes where provided. Clutches of eggs can be quite large, up to seven in the Eastern Rosella and eight occasionally recorded in the Green.

> ### WHY ROSELLA?
> The name is a contraction of Rosehill, a Sydney suburb, given because the Eastern Rosella was common there.

The Eastern Rosella occurs in Tasmania and the south-east from about Adelaide to the Queensland/New South Wales border. It hybridises with the Pale-headed Rosella where their ranges meet in northern New South Wales.

The Pale-headed Rosella inhabits north-eastern New South Wales and eastern Queensland. Many young birds in southern Queensland have red colouring on the head, indicating past hybridisation with the Eastern Rosella.

The Green Rosella is confined to Tasmania. Young birds are greener than the adults.

Northern Rosella inhabits the Top End and Kimberley, from Karumba, Queensland, to Broome, Western Australia.

The Crimson Rosella has two basic colour variants, a crimson one in more humid areas and a yellow one in the drier Murray-Darling Rivers region, with intergrades between them in South Australia.

The Western Rosella is found in south-west Western Australia. The even more attractive males in the drier inland Salmon Gum country have extensive red feathering on the back. Females are less colourful.

Cuckoos

*A*ll of the Australian cuckoos are at least partly migratory, except possibly for the Chestnut-breasted Cuckoo of the Cape York Peninsula. Most individuals vacate the south in winter, moving further north, but some do remain all year round. Most cuckoos feed on invertebrates, particularly hairy caterpillars that are generally avoided by other birds – they are eviscerated before swallowing and the hairs are later coughed up in a 'fur-ball'. Most cuckoos are heard before they are seen, their call nothing like the European 'cuck-oo'; Australia's Fan-tailed has a descending trill and a mournful whistle 'wh-phweee'; the Pallid a loud whistle-like ascending scale; the koel has a penetrating 'ko-well'. When seen, the cuckoo is often perched on a dead stick in the open, where it can see what other birds are around.

Above: Female Western Spinebill (a honeyeater) feeding a young Pallid Cuckoo, eight times its weight; Left: Day-old Horsfield's Bronze-Cuckoo ejecting a Red-capped Robin's egg; Opposite above: The Pallid Cuckoo has a loud ascending call; Opposite below: Female Variegated Fairy-wren with Horsfield's Bronze-Cuckoo chick.

CUCKOO DOMINANCE
The cuckoo's egg generally hatches before those of the host and the seemingly helpless chick begins a drama that is repeated in parasitised nests throughout the woodlands, struggling to position each egg in turn between its stumpy wings and pushing it laboriously out of the nest.

During the breeding season males call loudly, marking out territories and attracting females. At this time, any patch of woodland may be home to as many as six cuckoo species. Females are observant and note any nest-building activities by potential hosts. When she judges the time is right she deposits an egg in the nest, sometimes removing one of the host's eggs. The male cuckoo may assist by distracting the owners of the nest. Host birds vigorously defend their territories against adult cuckoos, but ironically, feed young cuckoos as if they are their own progeny and defend them against intruders. While a chick is still small in the nest, it is possible to determine whether it is a cuckoo or not by looking at the toes – a cuckoo has two facing forward and two back – and the nostril which is slightly raised. Cuckoo fledglings have a persistent call that seems irresistible and other birds than the hosts have been observed feeding the imposter, even taking it over altogether. It is probable that young cuckoos imprint on their hosts and parasitise that species when breeding later.

Above: The Little Bronze-Cuckoo is migratory in the north and east, arriving in spring. The male of this pair (upper) is singing, a downward trill and a loud four-noted call. They parasitised nesting White-throated Gerygones in our neighbour's garden.

Channel-billed Cuckoo

Each spring the Channel-bill arrives from its wintering grounds to the north of Australia and immediately attracts attention due to its loud raucous calls. It is usually seen in pairs or small flocks that start checking out the breeding status of the birds that will host their young – crows and ravens, currawongs and magpies. When a suitable host has completed a nest and begun laying, the female cuckoo lays her own egg while the male distracts the legitimate owners. Most cuckoos lay only one egg per nest but the Channel-bill occasionally lays more over consecutive days – we have seen as many as four fledglings being fed by a host crow. Other cuckoo chicks, as soon as they hatch, eject the host's eggs or young, but Channel-bills don't.

Pheasant Coucal

Although related to cuckoos, coucals build their own nests and rear their own young. Not strong fliers they inhabit areas of long grass, feeding on large insects, small reptiles and frogs. Like cuckoos they have two toes on each foot directed forwards and two backwards – one of the hind-toes has a very long claw, possibly as an aid to clambering through course grasses. Their plumage is normally mottled browns, but in the breeding season they develop black heads and breasts.

Eastern Koel

The koel is another migratory cuckoo, arriving in spring and departing in autumn after breeding. The sexes are very different in plumage – the male (above) is black and the female is attractively barred and spotted. Females come in two varieties, one with a black head and the other, less common, with more rufous plumage and with a rufous head (centre). As soon as they arrive koels attract attention through their loud 'coo-eel' calls, uttered day and night, so they are not as popular a garden visitor as most birds. They also have a penchant for mulberries and grapes so are not exactly welcomed by all backyard horticulturalists. Although as adults they are largely vegetarian, as chicks they depend on whatever food their hosts provide, which is usually insects. The main host is the Magpie-lark, but they also parasitise large honeyeaters like friarbirds, wattlebirds and Blue-faced Honeyeaters, as well as more unusual hosts like the Black-faced Cuckoo-shrike. Young ones (below) have a different plumage to either adult but soon moult into a set of feathers similar to the female's.

WHAT IS A RAINBIRD?

Several migratory cuckoos, like the Eastern Koel and Channel-billed Cuckoo, arrive with the onset of the wet season and call loudly. There are those who believe the calls foretell rain, a supposition that doesn't stand up to objective scrutiny.

Fan-tailed Cuckoo

Choosing much smaller birds to parasitise, the Fan-tailed Cuckoo shows a preference for those that build dome-shaped nests close to the ground. The Brown Thornbill is a primary target but other thornbills, fairy-wrens, scrubwrens and warblers are also chosen. Less often birds that build open nests like robins and honeyeaters are used. The observant female cuckoo is probably aware of all the nests being built in its territory and takes care not to lay twice in any one nest. In well-vegetated gardens that provide sufficient cover for small birds to breed, cuckoos are likely to visit. This photo was taken in our garden, where a Willie Wagtail's nest was parasitised.

Brush Cuckoo

Midway in size between the Fan-tailed Cuckoo and the bronze-cuckoos, the Brush parasitises the same suite of small birds, both dome-nesters and cup-nesters, for whom there is no respite; a patch of woodland may contain five or six species of cuckoos all on the lookout for suitable nests, and there are instances of nests containing an egg of each the Brush and Fan-tailed. The juvenile Brush Cuckoo (left) is heavily barred, unlike the adult which has a grey head, buff breast and lack of any barring. While being fed, a young cuckoo will often hold out one wing, almost buffeting the host bird, as if warding off competitors for the food – very strange behaviour.

CUCKOO FEET
Cuckoos, like parrots, have the two outer toes on each foot directed backwards and the two central toes directed forward.

Horsfield's Bronze-Cuckoo

This small cuckoo parasitises a wide range of small birds, both dome-nest builders like the Variegated Fairy-wren (above), other fairy-wrens, scrub-wrens and warblers, and builders of cup-shaped nests like robins and flycatchers. It is more likely to be found in well-planted inland gardens that attract host birds than in coastal gardens.

Shining Bronze-Cuckoo

This iridescent cuckoo parasitises about 70 species of small birds, but the main hosts are the Brown and Yellow-rumped Thornbills. Two races of the Shining Bronze-Cuckoo can be observed in Australia, one a local partial-migrant that breeds in the east and south-west and the other a non-breeding passage migrant from New Zealand which arrives in the east in March–April and departs over the Tasman Sea during September–October.

Laughing Kookaburra

Popular backyard visitors, kookaburras endear themselves through their 'laughter' and ready acceptance of human interaction. They live in small family groups that strongly defend their territories against rival groups. The laughter is a declaration of territory, a very serious business, warning off any trespassing kookaburras from neighbouring territories. Reflections in windows will also trigger aggression, and individuals may crash into the glass with a hefty thump. Usually this occurs when there is a perch from which a bird can see its reflection, so the attacks on the window can be curtailed if the perch is removed. Favoured prey consists of worms, insects, lizards, snakes and small mammals such as mice. They nest co-operatively in tree hollows or arboreal termite mounds and will use nest boxes in the garden.

Sacred Kingfisher

A migrant in the south, the Sacred Kingfisher generally arrives in late August or September and leaves in March, heading into the tropics and the islands to the north. However these dates vary from year to year. Occasionally there are irruptions in the south and many more birds than usual turn up. Not all birds migrate, so occasional birds may be seen in winter. In Tasmania it appears to be a non-breeding summer migrant. In the garden it is susceptible to cats, as much of its food of insects, spiders and lizards is caught on the ground. Favourite items are cicadas, which may be detected by sound. Nesting tunnels are dug into arboreal termitaria, creek-banks or rotting wood, or in natural hollows in trees, usually eucalypts. Commonly three to five eggs are laid.

DO ALL KINGFISHERS FISH?
Most Australian kingfishers rarely catch fish. They are basically forest and woodland birds, feeding on invertebrates and reptiles.

Rainbow Bee-eater

Bee-eaters feed on flying insects, captured in the beak following an aerobatic pursuit, then carried back to a suitable perch. Stinging insects such as bees and wasps are favoured items of prey. To avoid being stung while swallowing, bee-eaters bang the captured insect on the perch and may actually rub it on the wood to release the venom. They do not capture enough hive bees to affect honey production. In the south they are migratory, arriving in spring and leaving in autumn. Nesting tunnels are dug in the ground, either in vertical banks or in level ground, usually with sandy soil. We have seen tunnels in suburban lawns.

Dollarbird

Another migratory bird, arriving in spring and leaving in autumn, the Dollarbird is a member of the roller family, so named because of their aerobatics in pursuit of flying insects, particularly cicadas. They also pursue flying ants on hot summer evenings when the male and female ants emerge for their mating flights; sometimes dozens of Dollarbirds will appear on such occasions. They favour exposed perches like dead tree-branches and utility wires. Very few individuals spend the winter in Australia, with most migrating north to New Guinea and Indonesia. They choose hollows in trees for breeding and lay three to five white eggs. A favoured hollow may be reused annually. A hollow in a tall tree in our neighbours' garden was used for many years.

Why are Some Birds Absent at Times?

A number of birds migrate regularly either to avoid cold weather or because food becomes more difficult for them to find at certain times of the year. There are several different sorts of migrants: firstly, those that leave the south for the winter months and relocate further north, in the case of certain honeyeaters and fantails; secondly, those that leave Australia for the islands to the north, in the case of some cuckoos, flycatchers, monarchs and kingfishers; thirdly, some birds are altitudinal migrants, like the Rose Robin and some Tasmanian birds, that leave the high country for the winter; lastly, some birds, including the Shining Bronze-Cuckoo, arrive for the winter months from New Zealand. Birds like the Scarlet Honeyeater are not regular migrants but move in response to the flowering seasons of nectar-rich plants, so they can turn up in the garden at any time. Many birds like waders arrive from the northern hemisphere for our summer but they are unlikely to visit gardens – the same applies to seabirds that circle our shores in winter.

Rose Robin, an altitudinal migrant.

Many Welcome Swallows leave Tasmania and the south-east in winter, heading further north.

Do Birds Mate for Life?

M ost birds form pair-bonds for the purpose of producing and rearing offspring. Some form permanent and stable relationships, staying together throughout the year and only acquiring another partner if the old one dies. Many mate up for only one season, then disperse when the young become independent, searching out either the same or another partner at the approach of the next breeding season. Numerous birds don't form partnerships at all – in these the female, in the case of bowerbirds, or the male in Emus, takes on the sole responsibility of rearing the young. Do birds have emotional attachments? Those who believe man alone is capable of emotion say no; those who have seen cockatoo-pairs mutually preening or miners gathered around a comrade dead on the road say yes.

Why do Birds Sing?

We enjoy the songs of birds – the carolling of magpies, the sweet cadences of warblers, the vigorous renditions of Brown Honeyeaters and Rufous Whistlers, the dawn-song of Pied Butcherbirds which is so like the opening bars of Beethoven's Fifth Symphony, and the laughter of kookaburras. But these songs are not for our enjoyment; they have a far more serious intent, a proclamation of territory, saying to other birds of the same species 'this is my patch of bush – keep out'. They are also uttered by males to let prospective mates know that they are available. Bowerbirds, as well as indulging in whisper-songs, will mimic birds of prey if they are disturbed at their bowers, possibly as a threat. Apart from songs, birds also have calls that serve a different purpose. Contact-calls let a mate or family group know where an individual is; alarm-calls alert others to the presence of predators like birds of prey and cats.

Juvenile Pied Butcherbird singing for joy.

WHISPER SONG
Some birds, like the juvenile butcherbird (above) as well as thornbills, silvereyes and others, have whisper-songs that include mimicry. While perched and relaxed, beaks barely open, they quietly sing and appear to have no other reason than an expression of well-being.

Why do Male Fairy-wrens Carry Petals?

Fairy-wrens occur in small groups that breed cooperatively. Generally there is a dominant female. An idyllic lifestyle? No – the male fairy-wren has a wandering eye and given the chance will mate with a female from a neighbouring group. To appear more enticing he can carry all or part of a flower petal in his beak. The female he is trying to entice is all too willing, as DNA evidence reveals that the ploy is often successful. The irony is that each male fairy-wren is probably unwittingly rearing his neighbour's progeny.

Male Splendid Fairy-wren.

Superb Fairy-wren

Voted Australia's favourite bird in a survey conducted by *Australian Birdlife* magazine, the Superb Fairy-wren is a regular visitor or resident in thickly planted gardens in the south-east and Tasmania. Usually occurring in small parties of up to half a dozen birds, they forage on the ground for insects and invertebrates. The group usually consists of a dominant female that does most of the nest-building and lays the eggs, a dominant male and a number of helpers which are mostly brown like the female. Observation has shown that males often mate with neighbouring females. Nests are dome-shaped and well hidden in bushes.

Variegated Fairy-wren

These attractive birds are found over most of Australia except southern Victoria and south-west Western Australia. Like other fairy-wrens they occur in parties – this pair in our garden was accompanied by two other males and one female. We have occasionally seen groups of seven or eight birds. They require plenty of cover, so are only likely in densely planted gardens with plenty of undergrowth. Lantana thickets are favoured habitats. They nest two or three times a year usually rearing three chicks each time, feeding them on insects and spiders. Predation on the young must be quite heavy because the family parties don't seem to get much bigger over time. Cuckoos do parasitise nests, particularly Horsfield's Bronze-Cuckoo.

Red-backed Fairy-wren

Preferring long grasses, particularly where intermingled with shrubs and lantana, Red-backed Fairy-wrens occur over eastern and northern Australia, from about Port Stephens, New South Wales, to Broome, Western Australia. They travel in small groups, usually with only one fully-coloured male, although two have been reported occasionally. The dominant female builds the dome-shaped nest in tall grasses and does most of the incubation of three or four eggs. Nests are very well hidden but are occasionally parasitised by cuckoos. Once the eggs hatch, the male and other members of the group help the female to feed the chicks.

Splendid Fairy-wren

A party of Splendid Fairy-wrens is more likely to include a number of fully-coloured males than those of other species. For instance, we saw one nest in Western Australia being attended by five males as well as females. Such large numbers of birds cooperating in the rearing of young obviously has an influence on successful outcomes, as territorial defence as well as provision of food for chicks is shared. One theory suggests such behaviour is a response to the number of cuckoos in Australia. However, female cuckoos do often parasitise this species as well as other cooperative breeders. A number of subspecies occur, differing mainly in the colour of the male's breast and the intensity of the blue colouration. It is most likely to visit well-planted gardens in the south-west and arid interior, basically occurring west of the range of the Superb Fairy-wren, in deserts as well as the forested south-west. The dome-shaped nest is well hidden in dense shrubbery.

RODENT WRENS
Breeding fairy-wrens will lead intruders away from the nest with distraction displays such as the 'broken wing act' or 'the rodent run', where the wren stretches out horizontally and scuttles through the undergrowth.

White-throated Gerygone

The White-throated Gerygone utters an elfin falling cascade of notes. It inhabits the eastern and northern woodlands from about Adelaide, South Australia, to Broome, Western Australia. Much of its insect food is taken while hovering near leaves. It is most likely to visit outer suburban and country gardens well planted with eucalypt and acacia trees. Two or three freckled pink eggs are laid. It is one of the main hosts of the Little Bronze-Cuckoo: this nest for instance contained a cuckoo chick.

> **GERYGONE?**
> Ger - i - gon - ee (not pronounced Jer -) Gerygones are small warbler-like birds. The name is derived from Greek and means 'born of sound' – a reference to their sweet songs.

Yellow-rumped Thornbill

A number of thornbill species inhabit Australia. Some have brightly coloured rump-feathers, either chestnut, buff or yellow. The Yellow-rumped Thornbill has the brightest plumage and is a tame confiding bird. Much of its insect food is taken on the ground where it progresses jerkily like a clockwork toy. While resting in trees and shrubs, it

has the unique habit of periodically falling backwards on the perch. It builds a very large untidy domed nest, usually placed in a drooping spray of leaves. A unique feature is a false cup on top, thought by some, without much evidence, to fool cuckoos into laying there instead of in the internal nest-chamber. It doesn't work if that is the intention, because the Yellow-rumped Thornbill is heavily parasitised by a number of cuckoo species, from the large Fan-tailed to the small Horsfield's.

Brown and Striated Thornbills

The ranges of a number of similar thornbill species cover the southern two-thirds of Australia, the Brown (top) in the east, with a rusty forehead, the Inland, west of the Divide, with a freckled forehead and the Striated (left) with a streaked forehead. They have red or dark brown eyes. In drier areas lives the similar Chestnut-rumped which has a white eye. They feed on insects usually gleaned among leaves in the lower story but the Striated tends to feed higher in bushes and trees. The Brown and Inland are excellent mimics, including disproportionately loud calls of birds such as goshawks and cuckoos. The Striated is very noisy and a small party of half a dozen make the bush or garden seem full of birds. All build domed nests, either well hidden in grasses and shrubbery (Brown and Inland) or in outer foliage (Striated).

Weebill

Widely distributed wherever there are trees, from desert to forest, the Weebill is reputedly the smallest Australian bird (emu-wrens' bodies are smaller but they have longer tails). The short stubby beak is well adapted to taking thrips and lerps from leaves, mainly eucalypts. In the south birds are browner, becoming progressively more yellow northwards. This bird was in Tennant Creek, Northern Territory. The nest is dome-shaped, built among drooping outer leaves in eucalypts.

White-browed Scrubwren

This reclusive species requires dense undergrowth, so will only occur in well-planted gardens like the Canberra Arboretum where it is one of the commonest birds. It generally keeps under cover but will emerge onto lawns if undisturbed, searching for its insect and invertebrate prey. The large dome-shaped nest is particularly well-hidden, on or close to the ground, yet still manages to be parasitised by ever-alert cuckoos.

Honeyeaters

*H*oneyeaters represent the largest family of Australian birds – about 75 species – and inhabit areas from the most arid desert gibbers to the densest rainforests. All rely on nectar to a greater or lesser extent as an item of diet (varying from 25–80 per cent of intake), and have a brush-like tip to the tongue to facilitate efficient garnering from flowers. The length and curve of the beak gives some indication of floral preferences. Such a sugar-rich diet induces a high level of activity and many species are very aggressive and quarrelsome, some like the Noisy Miner to an excessive degree. Insects, invertebrates, manna, sap and fruits are also eaten, including lerps that develop a sugary shell on leaves and bark. Nearly all build suspended cup-shaped nests. One species, the Banded, nests in loose colonies, and some like the miners are cooperative breeders. The rare Square-tailed Kite appears to be a specialised honeyeater predator.

POLLINATION

Honeyeaters have a close association with nectar-producing flowers, and are important pollinators of many Australian native plants – the pollen being deposited on the birds' foreheads and passed from flower to flower.

Best Plants to Attract Honeyeaters

Many species are easily attracted to the garden with plantings of native flowering shrubs. The most useful are eucalypts, grevilleas, banksias, callistemons, eremophilas, kangaroo paws and heaths. Grevilleas are especially appropriate because there are many species, varieties and cultivars that come in an assortment of colours, sizes and shapes that can fit into any niche in the garden.

Clockwise from top right: Blue-faced Honeyeater on banksia; Eastern Spinebill on grevillea; Scarlet Honeyeater on callistemon; Fuchsia Heath; Red Wattlebird on Illyarrie Gum; Dusting of pollen on Lewin's Honeyeater.

Their true value is the fact that many have extended flowering periods, some all year, and they begin producing flowers quickly after planting. Some interesting grevilleas that might otherwise be difficult to maintain are grafted onto more robust stock. To discourage miners, the best varieties are those with smaller flowers requiring long beaks to reach the nectar (middle right). Some of the most popular cultivars, like Robin Gordon are miner-magnets. Banksias (now including the dryandras) also occur in a variety of shapes and sizes, from prostrate ground cover to small trees, and are very popular, with some honeyeaters feeding, nesting and roosting in one species. Probably the most spectacular is *Banksia coccinea*, but each species has its own character. Many forms are native to southern Western Australia and most of them are not suitable for subtropical and tropical gardens, but do well in drier temperate areas. In the east the various cultivars of *Banksia spinulosa* are worthy of places in any garden, and dried flower cones of *Banksia serrata* provide 'fur' to line nests. The many species of callistemons flower heavily but for short periods. Correas and other heaths attract long-billed honeyeaters. Eremophilas are attractive dry-country plants found throughout the inland, now available in a variety of cultivars, and once established they require a minimum of water.

CO-DEPENDENCE

Some honeyeaters time their breeding season to coincide with the flowering of particular nectar-rich plants such as banksias. This allows them to quickly feed themselves, then search for protein-rich food for their chicks. In return they pollinate the plants.

Lewin's Honeyeater

Generally solitary and common in rainforests and closed woodlands in the east from southern Victoria to Cooktown, Queensland, Lewin's Honeyeater is known for its machine-gun-like call. It is inquisitive and regularly visits gardens to harvest ripe fruit, both native and exotic, its primary food source; it also takes insects from foliage and tree trunks and nectar from a wide range of flowers, but perhaps favouring grevilleas. Like all honeyeaters it is an important pollinator and is often seen with a dusting of pollen on the forehead. Watch for birds carrying grass and moss as this indicates that they are nest-building. The untidy cup-shaped nest, bound with cobweb, is usually well hidden in dense foliage. The normal clutch is two eggs, three in a very good season.

White-plumed Honeyeater

With a range extending from the south-east through the centre to the mid-west, this honeyeater is common wherever there are eucalypts and access to water: it is probably the commonest bird of tree-lined channels in the inland. In the garden, they will be attracted to water and are very fond of bathing. The plumage in the south-east has a greenish tinge; further west and north (left) it becomes progressively more yellow. They live in small colonies and are quite noisy,

their call a pleasant, variable 'chick-o-wee'. Gardeners enjoy having these birds around as they forage mainly in foliage and eat many insects – ants, flies, aphids and lerps, as well as spiders – berries and nectar are also favoured. The beaks in non-breeding birds (bottom left) have a yellow base and black tip, while the beaks of breeding birds are all black (middle left). The nest is built in drooping eucalypt leaves. At one nest chicks were fed 40 times in 30 minutes by three adults.

Singing Honeyeater

Widely spread west of the Divide,
the Singing Honeyeater appears to
be increasing in numbers in many
localities. Not a very melodious songster,
it is a common garden bird in the west,
particularly in the south-west. Nectar
forms about 25 per cent of its diet, with the
remainder insects and some fruit. It nests in
low shrubbery, mainly between September
and January, but in the desert may nest
after rain. Usually two eggs are laid.

Yellow-faced Honeyeater

A common honeyeater in eastern forests
and woodlands from about Adelaide
to Cooktown. A partial migrant, with
most leaving the south-east in April and
returning from July–October, wintering
in north-eastern New South Wales and
eastern Queensland. During migration
flocks travel noisily from tree to tree.
Nectar forms 10–20 per cent of its diet;
insects are mostly gleaned from leaves,
some are taken in the air. The typical
honeyeater nest is usually in a low bush,
housing two or three eggs.

Macleay's Honeyeater

This attractive honeyeater has a restricted
range in northern Queensland, from about
Cardwell to Cooktown. Usually observed
singly or in pairs, occasionally in small
flocks. As well as nectar, it feeds on insects,
often searching tree-trunks and dead leaves;
fruit such as native figs also features in the
diet. Nests are sometimes built in tangled
vines higher than most honeyeaters, and
are deep suspended cups.

White-naped Honeyeater

Another partial migrant in the south-east the White-naped Honeyeater moves north in winter, returning in spring. In the west a similar bird, the Western Honeyeater, doesn't appear to migrate – it has a white wattle over the eye, but otherwise looks and behaves much the same. Both feed often in small flocks, mostly in eucalypts, foraging among leaves for insects, leaf-galls, manna, lerps and sap as well as nectar in flowers.

White-throated Honeyeater

Superficially similar to the White-naped, the White-throated has a whitish wattle over the eye and lacks any black under the chin; its call is peevish and penetrating, while the White-naped's is sibilant. It occurs from north-eastern New South Wales to about Broome, Western Australia. It moves in small flocks and, like the White-naped, breeds cooperatively. The suspended cup-nest is built in a drooping clump of eucalypt leaves, and the chicks are fed by several adults.

Crescent Honeyeater

The Crescent Honeyeater appears to be an altitudinal migrant in Tasmania and the south-east, leaving high country in winter. It is common in woodland and heaths, and feeds equally between insects and nectar. The female builds the nest, usually well hidden in shrubbery, and incubates the two spotted pink eggs. If the nest is approached she may perform a distraction display. The male assists in feeding the young. Enjoys bathing in hot weather.

Blue-faced Honeyeater

Ranging in eastern and northern woodlands from about Adelaide to Broome, the Blue-faced Honeyeater comes in two varieties, one in the east with a buff patch in the wing and the other in the north with a white patch; the bare skin on the face and the beaks are slightly different too. Adults (inset) have beautiful blue bare skin; in young birds it is greenish or yellowish (left). Food consists of nectar, fruit and insects. Insects are often gleaned from bark. Usually occurs in small flocks and breeds cooperatively. Nests are often built in the base of palm-tree fronds, but they will also use old babbler stick-nests. They are one of the hosts of the Eastern Koel.

New Holland Honeyeater

This honeyeater is similar to the White-cheeked, which has a dark eye and a larger white ear-patch. In many areas they appear to be more dependant on nectar than other honeyeaters, with this comprising up to 80 per cent of intake. They are partial to banksias and will defend flowers in their territories. They prefer dense shrubbery and will visit well-planted gardens in the south-east and south-west, particularly if banksias or dryandras are present. The nest is well hidden in shrubbery and contains two or three spotted pinkish eggs, usually in late winter. Young are fed on nectar and insects. One would think such a diet would discourage cuckoos but both Pallid and Horsfield's have been found in nests.

Noisy Friarbird

Well-named, Noisy Friarbirds keep up a constant cackling while feeding. Often aggressive, they seem to burn off excess energy with busy quarrels, chasing other honeyeaters as well. About half of their food intake is nectar, while insects and fruit constitute the other half. In the south-east they are partly migratory, heading north in March and returning in August–September. The nest is an untidy basket in a horizontal fork.

Little Friarbird

Partly migratory in the south-east, the Little Friarbird is often considered to be nomadic over its range in the east and north, but it is more likely that it responds locally to flower availability. Although aggressive to other species, driving them away from favoured flowers, it seems to respect the Noisy Friarbird. The nest is a woven basket slung in a horizontal tree-fork in a eucalypt or paperbark. Two or three eggs form the clutch.

Helmeted Friarbird

Confined to north-eastern Queensland and the Top End, Northern Territory, the Helmeted Friarbird comes in three varieties, differing in the shape and size of the casque on the beak. This is the Queensland form. The other two are found in the Northern Territory, one in sandstone country and the other in coastal mangroves and woodlands. Perhaps three species are involved. The smaller Silver-crowned Friarbird co-exists with them.

Miners

Opinions are divided about miners. On one hand, they are extremely interesting birds living in groups that cooperate in breeding and vigorously defending territories, have a varied vocabulary of calls and songs and have complex behaviour. On the other hand, they are so aggressive in defending their territories that they will drive other species away, so a garden planted in such a way as to encourage miners will attract few other birds. There are four miners; the Noisy (above) in the east, the Yellow-throated (below) west of the Divide, the Bell Miner in south-eastern forests,

and the endangered Black-eared Miner in the eastern mallee. The Noisy and Yellow-throated regularly visit gardens. They favour those that are planted with grevilleas and callistemons and little understory, such as one finds in many public parks and gardens. The denser the planting the less likely miners are to visit. Where they are a problem there are two alternatives: plant more densely to provide refuges, or remove the birds by culling. The latter alternative, illegal at the moment, has been shown to work in trials. We think the former is a better solution in public gardens. In private gardens the planting solution is most likely to work if other gardens in the vicinity follow suit.

LIVING WITH MINERS
Birds that can co-exist with miners are Crested Pigeons, brush-turkeys, Magpie-larks, magpies and butcherbirds. Kookaburras are regularly harassed but will still come in for hand-outs.

Scarlet Honeyeater

Basically nomads, Scarlet Honeyeaters follow the flowering of eucalypts and melaleucas. Some years they will arrive in large numbers and at other times not at all, even though the flowering seems the same. They regularly visit gardens that feature grevilleas, callistemons, eucalypts and euodias. During summer they will utilise watering points in the garden, sometimes a dozen or more drinking at the same time.

Brown Honeyeater

A common visitor or resident in gardens throughout much of Australia, excepting the deserts and the south-east, the Brown Honeyeater has a sweet song, much more melodious than the Singing Honeyeater (page 59). About 60 per cent of food is nectar, the rest insects, taken among leaves or in the air. A small cup-shaped nest is well hidden in shrubbery or vines, usually within a metre of the ground. This male spent much time singing near the nest.

Dusky Honeyeater

Often feeding with Brown and Scarlet Honeyeaters, the Dusky occupies forests and paperbark woodlands in eastern Queensland and the Top End. Like many honeyeaters it is aggressive and spends time chasing and quarrelling with beak-snaps. The nest is a rather flimsy cup suspended in outer foliage. Two spotted and blotched white eggs are laid. Distraction displays may be given if the nest is disturbed.

Spinebills

Spinebills will often hover while they are exploring flowers for nectar. Forests, heaths and woodlands with dense understories are favoured habitats of the Eastern Spinebill (top right) particularly where there are banksias, bottle-brushes and heaths, ranging from about Adelaide to Cooktown in the east and in Tasmania. A large percentage of the diet is nectar. It regularly visits

gardens well planted with native flowers. Nests from August–April; two to four broods may be reared each year. The Western Spinebill (right), inhabiting the south-west, favours banksias but also visits other flowers including eucalypts and kangaroo paws. The male has an attractive display-flight, flying straight up and plummeting back to cover. Territory is vigorously defended from other spinebills. Nesting usually occurs from September–December. In our garden at Kelmscott, Western Australia, a pair reared a Pallid Cuckoo. As the insects they caught were small one wonders how they satisfied the very large chick about eight times heavier than the spinebills.

> **NOISY TAKE-OFF**
> Spinebills make their presence known in the garden with the loud fluttering made by their wings in flight. Other small honeyeaters also flutter but not as loudly as spinebills.

Rufous-banded Honeyeater

Confined to northern Queensland and the Top End, this honeyeater prefers paperbark woodlands, making frequent forays to flowering eucalypts. Common in Darwin gardens, one banded bird lived at least nine years. The similar Rufous-throated Honeyeater (page 13) is more widely spread in the north. Both build hanging deep purse-like nests which often get soaked in the wet season but quickly dry out. Both lay two white eggs freckled with brown and purple.

Little Wattlebird

Neither the Little Wattlebird (above) nor the Western (below) have wattles, but in other respects they are similar in diet and behaviour to their larger wattled relatives. The Little occupies the south-east from about Adelaide to near Seventeen Seventy, Queensland, as well as Tasmania. It has a grey or grey-blue eye and attractively streaked plumage. The calls are raucous and incessant while feeding, principally in banksias and grevilleas, but on insects as well. When flying ants are emerging it flies up to take them in the air. The nest is well concealed in a shrub, vine or low tree.

Western Wattlebird

Confined to the south-west in open forest and woodland preferably with an understory of banksias or dryandras, the Western Wattlebird has a red or reddish-brown eye and a longer, finer bill than the Little, probably a reflection of a different suite of banksias. While calling it has the typical wattlebird habit of throwing the head back. In some areas up to 80 per cent of food intake is nectar, with the remainder insects. The nest is rather shallow, usually well hidden; prickly dryandras (left) are often chosen as nest sites. The eggs are pinkish-buff with darker speckles and blotches. Both adults feed the chicks.

Red Wattlebird

A regular visitor to parks and gardens across southern Australia from the Murchison River, Western Australia, to Cooloola, Queensland, the Red Wattlebird favours woodlands and heaths with understories including banksias. It also visits flowering eucalypts like the Illyarrie (see page 58). In the past it was considered a pest in orchards and shot accordingly (and eaten!), but it usually only attacks over-ripe fruit. It has increased in numbers around Sydney and Adelaide, some say to the detriment of other birds in the latter. Sometimes

an individual will defend a whole flowering tree, driving other nectar-eaters away. 60–70 per cent of the diet appears to be nectar, the rest consisting of manna, insects, including lerps, and some fruits. The calls are loud and cackling, uttered vigorously with the head thrown back. The nest is built in tall shrubs or trees and usually hidden among leaves. At one nest the parents fed the chicks 40 times in an hour from nectar collected from prostrate dryandras near the nest.

Yellow Wattlebird

Like other honeyeaters Yellow Wattlebirds of Tasmania and King Island are aggressive, disputing access to flowers. Insects and fruit are also consumed. In the 1890s 'hundreds of thousands' were reported in one area and they were commonly shot. Although now protected it has probably not returned to its former numbers in woodlands and forests. Resident in some areas, in others it arrives in response to flowering of banksias and eucalypts and visits gardens, mainly in autumn and winter. Large loose cup-nests are built in trees or shrubs and not always hidden from view. Two or three lightly blotched pinky buff eggs are laid.

WATTLEBIRD PIE?
In times past the Yellow Wattlebird was listed as a gamebird in Tasmania, and until about 1970 was shot for consumption. The Red Wattlebird was also eaten in smaller numbers.

Why do Male Bowerbirds Build Bowers?

*M*ost birds form pair-bonds to breed. In some, both sexes share nesting duties and in others most of the nest-building and incubation is done by the female while she is fed by her mate. In a few, like button-quails and emus, the role of the sexes is reversed, with the male making the nest, incubating the eggs and caring for the young. Some birds don't form pair-bonds at all but use other strategies to bring male and female together for mating. One of the most interesting is the use of 'play-grounds', or bowers, by male bowerbirds to attract females for mating. There are three main types of bowers: simple clearings decorated with leaves; avenues; and maypoles. The one most likely to be constructed in or near gardens is the avenue bower, like the structures above and right, with male bowerbirds adding twigs or grass-stems to the bower walls. The building and maintenance of a bower takes a lot of time and energy and is only possible if there is easily available food, rainforest fruits like the satinwood for the Satin Bowerbird (right), berries and seeds like wilga for the Spotted Bowerbird (above) and rock figs for the Western Bowerbird (top right).

Adding Ornaments

*O*nce the bower is built the male adds ornaments; most are placed at the northern end of the bower, and some favoured items are placed inside the bower walls. The Satin Bowerbird favours blue ornaments including feathers, flowers and household items like clothes-pegs; Spotted and Western Bowerbirds favour white bones, pebbles and green berries. The Western also adds green leaves (right), possibly for the contrast afforded to the lilac-coloured nape during displays. A lot of time is spent by the male arranging, rearranging

and replacing the ornaments and in performing vigorous displays. Observations suggest that a visiting female standing in the bower sees the arranged ornaments and the display to their best advantage.

Painting the Bower

*E*ven more remarkable than the construction and decoration of bowers is the fact that the male 'paints' the sticks or grass-stems making up the bower walls with a paste of vegetable material. The large southern Satin Bowerbird (right) frequently uses hoop-pine leaves while the smaller northern birds often use tobacco bush berries. The Western Bowerbird uses a variety of paints including over-ripe rock figs and possibly even large ants. Female bowerbirds

are probably aware of all the bowers in their vicinity and visit them all before deciding which male to mate with. The female has a choice of whether or not to mate because of the design of the bower – she enters from the southern end and the male displays in front of the northern end. To mate he has to hop around to the southern end to approach the female from behind, affording her an opportunity to escape through the front if she decides not to consummate.

> **BUSH ARTIST**
> Many male birds feed their mates during courtship. Bowerbird males don't, but perhaps, when they are painting bower walls, they are symbolically feeding females.

Green Catbird

The catbird is basically a bowerbird that doesn't build a bower, nor does it have specialised displays. It is found in or near rainforests, from south-eastern New South Wales to southern Queensland. In north-eastern Queensland its place is taken by the Spotted Catbird, which is similar but with a black ear-patch. Catbirds usually keep well hidden in the canopy but reveal their presence with loud cat-like meows. They feed on fruits, mainly native figs, but also take insects, frogs, and occasional small birds. They will visit gardens near rainforest. Nests

are built in upright forks or in tree-ferns, one to three glossy cream eggs are laid. The female builds the nest, incubates the eggs and broods the young; males assist in feeding chicks.

Satin Bowerbird

Ranging discontinuously from about the Otway Ranges, Victoria, to the Seaview Range, Queensland, the Satin Bowerbird is a common visitor to gardens. The male constructs a bower with upright twigs forming an avenue on a platform, which is decorated with such items as blue feathers and flowers, yellow leaves, native pine leaves and cicada exoskeletons. Blue pegs are a favoured adornment. Males spend a lot of time arranging and rearranging the bower and may 'paint' the walls with a paste of masticated fruits. Males acquire blue plumage at about six years of age. Young males are green like the females, and construct rudimentary

bowers; it seems to take a few years of practice to become proficient builders. The main items of diet are fruits, but flowers, insects, particularly cicadas, and occasional fledglings are also eaten. Nesting is left to the female; she builds a well-hidden cup-shaped nest in an upright fork.

Spotted Bowerbird

Although widely spread and common in dry woodlands in inland New South Wales and Queensland, the Spotted Bowerbird is becoming scarce in the south, endangered in Victoria and extinct in South Australia. Males build larger bowers than the Satin Bowerbird, nearly always oriented north to south, They also add more adornments, usually white bones and stones, green berries, callitris leaves and broken glass. Most items are placed at the northern end of the bower with a little heap of 'treasures' between the walls, which are mostly formed from grass-stems backed by twigs. Females probably visit all the bowers in their area before deciding which male to mate with. They perform all nesting duties without any help from males.

> **IS THE BOWER A NEST?**
> No, bowers are display grounds where males court females. Cup-shaped nests are built by females and are well-hidden in trees.

Western Bowerbird

This bowerbird replaces the Spotted in the centre and west, principally in the central ranges and in the mid west, extending to North-west Cape, Western Australia. It is associated with the native rock fig, but also moves into dry woodlands away from the

ranges. Visits outback gardens and is common around Alice Springs. Bowers are similar to those of the Spotted, but tend to be built on a bigger platform and with more decorations. Immature males often visit bowers and will display, arrange items and even 'paint' the walls, usually while the owner is absent. Females build cup-shaped nests, often in mistletoe clumps, and perform all nesting duties without help from males.

Black-faced Cuckoo-shrike

Cuckoo-shrikes are neither cuckoos nor shrikes, so named because of a fancied resemblance to both. The Black-faced occurs all over Australia and Tasmania wherever there are trees. It feeds on the fruit of plants like mulberry and tobacco bush, and on large insects including

destructive phasmids. One in our yard fed a Peaceful Dove's egg to its chick. The smaller White-bellied Cuckoo-shrike of the east and north occasionally visits gardens well planted with trees. The black on its head is confined to the area in front of the beak; in immature Black-faced the black extends as a mask behind the eye. Both make small nests on horizontal forks.

Grey Shrike-thrush

A regular visitor to gardens with remnant vegetation throughout Australia and Tasmania, the Grey Shrike-thrush is likely to attack windows if there are perches positioned so that reflections are visible, usually in the breeding season, August–December in the south, February–April in the north. Females have faint streaking on the throat and breast; in young birds the streaking is darker and more extensive, and they have a rufous eyebrow and edges to the wing-feathers. Shrike-thrushes feed

mainly on insects but will catch small vertebrates including frogs, birds and even Feather-tailed Gliders; they also take seeds, flowers and fruit. Nests are usually placed in upright tree-hollows but individuals will also use odd sites in the garden like hanging baskets and old letter-boxes.

HYPHENATED NAMES
Some Australian birds have double-banger names, like Shrike-thrush and Bronze-Cuckoo. A Shrike-thrush is not a thrush so it doesn't have a capital letter. A Bronze-Cuckoo is a cuckoo so it has a capital.

Rufous Whistler

A vigorous songster, the Rufous Whistler often responds to a sudden noise such as a car-door slamming. Its repertoire is rich and varied; one of its calls is a rapidly repeated series based on the often heard 'eechong'; we once heard a male utter 50 repetitions. Generally older males have a more complex vocabulary than young ones, mixing and matching different elements of song. Females and young are quite different in plumage with streaked underparts, rather like young shrike-thrushes. Food consists mainly of insects, usually taken in foliage higher than other whistlers; occasionally fruit and seeds are consumed. The nest is rather sparse, usually placed in a fork, not necessarily hidden in foliage. Males may breed while still in immature plumage.

Golden Whistler

The song of the Golden Whistler is a series of four or five sweet notes followed by a whip-crack; other calls include a soft 'seet', but are not nearly as complex as those of the Rufous Whistler. Females are rather like female Rufous Whistlers but lack any streaking on the breast, Juveniles are rufous but quickly moult to immature plumage which is like the female but with retained juvenile rufous wing-feathers (lower right). Females often have yellow undertail-coverts. They occupy forests and woodlands in eastern and southern Australia and Tasmania, particularly in moist environments with dense understory. Food consists mainly of insects. The nest is usually well-hidden in a shrub, vine or small tree, usually in the outer foliage with two to three blotched and spotted eggs.

Robins

*A*ustralasian robins have no relationship with robins in other places like Europe and America. The name was first applied to the Scarlet Robin by early settlers nostalgic for the 'robin redbreast' (European Robin) back in Britain. In Australia there are five species in which males have red or pink breasts. Several have yellow breasts in males and females, and several have uncoloured breasts. The Red-capped Robin and Jacky Winter are the most widespread, occurring in woodlands throughout much of the drier regions. Others are more restricted in range; the Dusky Robin for instance is confined to Tasmania, which it shares with the more widespread Scarlet and Flame Robins. Most of them feed on insects in a similar manner, sitting on a low perch then flying down to take their prey on the ground, but they will also glean insects from tree-trunks and leaves. The Rose Robin (see page 52) is more arboreal and often hovers flycatcher-fashion at a clump of leaves. It was a regular visitor to our garden until Noisy Miners invaded. Several species briefly open the wings to flush their quarry and will also watch gardeners, swooping down to pick up disturbed invertebrates. Nests are deep cups placed in a tree-fork, usually vertical but sometimes on horizontal forks. They are usually well decorated with bark or lichen to simulate the surroundings; some of them to human eyes are very beautiful, the Rose Robin's in particular. The Jacky Winter's nest is the smallest made by any Australian bird.

COURTSHIP FEEDING
At the onset of the breeding season, male robins feed their mates; females solicit with quivering wings as the male approaches. Feeding continues until the eggs hatch, after which both sexes feed the chicks.

The Western Yellow Robin's range extends from south-west Western Australia into South Australia.

The Eastern Yellow Robin occurs from eastern South Australia to Cooktown, Queensland.

The Scarlet Robin occurs in the south-east, south-west and in Tasmania. The female is brown with a pinkish breast and white flashes in the wings.

The Dusky Robin is confined to Tasmania and Bass Strait islands. Its plain colouration is probably similar to that of ancestral robins.

The Red-capped Robin is found over the drier southern three-quarters of Australia.

The Jacky Winter is widespread in woodlands throughout Australia.

Figbird

Figbirds come in two colour varieties, one with grey and olive underparts in the south and a yellow-breasted form in the north. In both the males have red 'spectacles', but the colour can change to pale orange, particularly when approaching the nest. They feed on fruit including native figs, palms, mulberries, chillies and asparagus fern. They often nest in loose colonies, with much noisy stealing of nest material.

Olive-backed Oriole

Orioles are related to figbirds but are more elegantly proportioned. They too feed on fruit, often with figbirds, but a proportion of their diet is insects and other invertebrates, and nectar. Their range is from the south-east to the Kimberley. They call frequently and are given to mimicry; an individual may mimic as many as a dozen species during a song-cycle. The nest is a substantial cup suspended in a horizontal tree-fork.

Apostlebird

These sociable birds live in small tightly-knit flocks of about a dozen birds, hence the name. They have a strong smell that probably aids bonding and they spend a lot of time perched together, mutually preening. They range through the interior of the eastern states, but there are some isolated groups that visit gardens in Brisbane outer suburbs. In country towns they soon learn where seed is provided.

Butcherbirds

Three species of butcherbird regularly visit gardens and soon learn to arrive when the lawn is being mown to glean disturbed insects, spiders and frogs. Common throughout the southern two-thirds of Australia (further north in Queensland) the Grey Butcherbird (right) is replaced by the similar Silver-backed Butcherbird in Northern Territory and the Kimberley. Both feed on invertebrates as well as small vertebrates like lizards, mice and small birds, including nestlings. The nests of all butcherbirds are shallow cups in trees rarely at any great height, and are vigorously defended, even from humans. Widespread in open forests and woodlands throughout most of Australia, the Pied Butcherbird (below) is absent from the arid areas of South Australia. Young birds are brown and white, moulting to pied at about 11 months. Common garden residents, Pieds add handouts to the normal diet of invertebrates and small vertebrates. At our place Grey Butcherbirds live on one side of the house, Pieds on the other – we have seen only one interaction between them in 40 years.

GARDEN BUTCHER SHOP
Any items of food too large to swallow whole are wedged by butcherbirds into suitable crevices or onto thorns to aid the stripping of suitably-sized portions, basically as an aid to feeding but also as a 'larder' to store food. If fed too much at the feeding table they will carry the excess away to be stored and eaten later.

Australian Magpie

Clearing in Australia has benefited the magpie; its preferred habitat is grassland with scattered trees for roosting and nesting, so agricultural land and park and garden lawns alike provide ideal conditions. Generally they reside in defended territories in pairs or small groups averaging seven in the lower south, and three to five elsewhere. Disputes often occur where territories abut, or when males from outside attempt to mate with resident females. However it is often difficult to tell whether interactions are serious, because resident birds often indulge in play-fighting. Judging from the female's puff-posture above, that interaction was territorial, the bird on its back showing submissive behaviour; the fight pictured opposite top, witnessed by other birds, was probably play. It's fun to watch young birds play – they pounce on and grab objects such as leaves or clothes pegs, then roll around on their backs kicking and pecking that object – they play in a similar manner with their siblings, the adults sometimes joining in. Both male (white nape) and female (grey nape) sing their beautiful carolling song, often in duet. The young birds, with beaks almost closed, quietly practice their song.

Magpies only attack during nesting season (June–December), vigorously defending their eggs and chicks from any possible threat. Humans, cats, dogs or any other bird that gets too close often end up with lumps taken out of them. Females do most of the nest-building, incubation and feeding of the chicks. After fledging, the whole group become involved in feeding the young. Nests are large cups often incorporating wire as well as sticks, and are situated at the top of fairly open, tall trees. The three to five eggs are pale blue or green with brown spots and streaks. Once the immatures (bottom right) become independent, they are aggressively evicted from the group. In the garden, Magpies spend most of their time on the lawn, searching for worms, snails, frogs, insects, lizards and mice as well as seed and fruit. They readily accept hand-outs of meat (with added calcium powder) and will also feed on seed.

SELECTIVE AGGRESSION
If magpies nest in your garden and you are often seen and don't interfere, they are unlikely to swoop at you, but if a stranger appears they will probably attack

Currawongs

Three currawong species inhabit eastern and southern Australia. In the east the Pied (left) is a regular garden visitor. It is not always welcomed because of predation on small nesting birds. Over the past 30 years it has increased in numbers in suburbs and towns. In the south-east, south, south-west and Tasmania lives the Grey Currawong; it is variable in colour, from black and white in Tasmania to grey and white in the west. Confined to Tasmania is the larger Black Currawong. All feed on insects, small vertebrates, fruit and seeds. Nests are usually placed in upright forks among leaves.

Magpie-lark

Found all over Australia wherever there are trees and water, Magpie-larks are common throughout the mainland, less so in Tasmania. They are regular visitors to gardens with expanses of lawn. (A male and a female are resident in our yard and find all the food they need in about two-thirds of an acre). Insects and seeds form the diet. When feeding they will often rotate on the spot, pattering with their feet. They persistently attack their reflections in windows of homes and cars, including wing-mirrors, particularly during the breeding season. As they may raise two or three broods a year

the windows are targeted for many months. Nests are made from mud, reinforced with grass and leaves picked up on the ground. The same site is often used for years. Other birds may use the nests once abandoned – frogmouths, doves and once even kestrels. Young stay with the adults for some weeks then disperse, sometimes joining flocks.

Corvids

Although there are five species of corvids in Australia, they are so similar in appearance that they are difficult to tell apart. Adults of all have white eyes; juveniles have blue eyes for a short time, changing to brown. Three are ravens, characterised by long hackles with grey bases on the throat, and two are crows, with short hackles having white bases, usually only visible in strong wind or when they preen. Locality is some help in identifying them: in the south-east only ravens occur, with the Little Raven and Forest Raven not extending further – the Forest Raven is the only corvid in Tasmania; it also occurs in a small number of forests in Victoria and northern New South Wales. Outside the south-east the Torresian Crow (centre), Little Crow and Australian Raven (top) are found. Some help in telling them apart is by listening to their calls. Basically crows are more nasal than ravens; the Forest Raven has the lowest call, the Little Crow and Little Raven are a step higher, and the Torresian is between them and the Australian Raven which is the highest. Unfortunately they all have variations and the young ones confuse the issue, so unless one is experienced it is better just to refer to those that visit as corvids, or seek advice from a birdwatcher. They are omnivorous with a large part of their diet comprised of carrion, but will accept seeds from the bird table. Generally they are wary but lose their fear in parks and gardens. At times they form noisy flocks. A bonded pair will start breeding in spring, building a large stick-nest at the top of a tall tree.

ARE CORVIDS INTELLIGENT?
Experiments with crows have shown that they can solve problems and learn from experience. For example, in one experiment a crow dropped stones into a beaker half-full of water to raise the level so it could reach floating food. Corvids have been known to use twigs to extract grubs from holes, and even to bend a piece of wire to make a hook to extract hidden insects.

Willie Wagtail

Ever watched a Willie Wagtail tormenting a pet cat? To humans it seems as if it is done just to annoy but it is actually a very serious activity – the wagtail knows the cat is a predator and is expressing its displeasure. It flutters just above the cat's head scolding with a distinctive chatter. Quite a number of black and white birds are similarly aggressive particularly in the breeding season when chicks need to be protected. Wagtails will also harass kookaburras, currawongs and any raptors that venture into the garden. They are quite tame and consume flying insects in the garden. They nest in spring and summer, often choosing positions on man-made structures and collecting cobwebs from under the eaves to build their nest. They will also choose sites near magpie or magpie-lark nests. Usually a number of broods are reared each year; the normal clutch is three.

> **NIGHT SONG**
> The Willie Wagtail's song is quite a pretty whistling chatter. If they roost near a streetlight, they sing through the night, annoying some insomniacs.

Restless Flycatcher

A harsh sound rather like an old-fashioned scissors-grinder sharpening cutlery alerts attention to the Restless Flycatcher. This call is often uttered while the bird is hovering in flight, searching the ground below or on hanging leaves for insects and spiders. It also has some sweeter songs including a loud penetrating 'towhee-towhee-towhee'. The nest, rather like a Willie Wagtail's, is usually placed on a horizontal branch and is often decorated with lichen. In the north its place is taken by the Paperbark Flycatcher.

Grey Fantail

Dynamically aerobatic, Grey Fantails catch insects in flight with ease, many of them very small. The long wide tail enables fantails to make abrupt turns while they pursue their quarry. They are partly migratory; while many remain at home most head north for winter. Those in Tasmania and Victoria head to New South Wales, replacing New South Wales birds that head to Queensland. Some Queensland birds make it as far as New Guinea. Further west many move into the inland and in winter the acacia woodlands are full of fantails' sweet calls and erratic gyrations. In gardens

they are more likely in winter; they don't visit feeding tables but will drink and bathe if water is provided, preferably above ground. They were regulars in our garden until miners moved into the neighbourhood. The nest is placed on a horizontal branch and, like other fantails, usually has a 'tail', probably to aid water run-off when it rains.

Rufous Fantail

Not quite as aerobatic as the Grey Fantail, the Rufous is still a very efficient gleaner of flying insects, sometimes sitting on the ground and sallying up to take choice items. It prefers denser habitats than the Grey, and is a common bird in rainforests as well as moist understory in eucalypt forests. It is more strictly migratory than the Grey, with most in the south-east leaving in March–April to head for north Queensland and New Guinea, returning in September–October. It is most likely to occur in the garden for a few days while on passage during those months. In the north a similar species, the Arafura Fantail, appears to be resident.

Silvereye

Common garden visitors, Silvereyes feed on insects, nectar, fruit and some seeds. Their pointy beak can drill a hole at the base of tubular flowers and their short brush-tipped tongue extracts the nectar. They can be quite destructive to garden fruit, but make up for it by eating aphids and other insect pests. They are partly migratory (one banded bird made it from south-west Western Australia to Sydney); many leave Tasmania and the south-east in autumn, returning in spring, but large numbers remain behind. In the east, backs are grey (above); in the west backs are olive (centre).

Mistletoebird

Mistletoe berries are the favoured food item of this tiny bird, but introduced plants like pepper trees are also harvested. The bird pictured here is sitting in characteristic fashion along the branch rather than across as other birds normally do. This enables excreted mistletoe berries to adhere to the branch, thus propagating this parasitic plant. It is perhaps worthwhile to leave mistletoes on any garden trees to attract these beautiful birds; unless the tree is sick, mistletoe is unlikely to kill it. The nest is a masterpiece, made from thistle-down and cobwebs, probably weighing less than the eggs that are laid in it.

Olive-backed Sunbird

Only male sunbirds have iridescent feathers on the throat and breast; in females and youngsters these feathers are yellow. They inhabit eastern Queensland northwards from about Gladstone, visiting flowers for nectar and searching for invertebrates, even entering homes in search of spiders. A wire with a hook or a rope hung up under the eaves may persuade a female to begin building a nest. Males assist in feeding the young.

Martins and Swallows

Martins have short rounded outer tail-feathers, while in swallows these feathers are long and thin. Otherwise they are similar in most respects. Welcome Swallows (centre right) frequently make use of urban buildings to build their cup-shaped mud-nests. For a few years we had three pairs nesting under our eaves and in the shed. As the chicks develop they squirt their droppings over the side of the nest; a board placed just under prevents an unsightly mess on the ground below. The number of insects they consume more than compensates for any inconvenience. Fairy Martins (lower right) are less likely to build under eaves, but when they do they form tightly-packed colonies of bottle-shaped mud-nests. We had about 30 on our front verandah and our neighbour had even more. The colony does tend to attract Brown Tree Snakes. Other birds like the Tree Martin and the White-backed Swallow are less likely to visit – both overfly our house frequently without ever landing.

> **ON THE WING**
> Martins and swallows do almost everything on the wing; eating insects, drinking (scooping up water over large dams) and even bathing.

Golden-headed Cisticola

If you are lucky enough to have cisticolas in your garden you probably don't have a lawnmower, because they are very much birds of long grass. They are only likely in large outer-suburban or country gardens. The nest, such as this one in our yard, is built inside a dome of leaves sewn together, using the beak as a needle and cobwebs for thread.

Pardalotes

Usually keeping to the treetops where they feed on lerps and other destructive insects, many pardalotes only come to ground when they are nesting. Spotted Pardalotes (below) invariably dig a tunnel into an earthen bank, a considerable effort; a nest is constructed mainly from strips of bark at the end of the tunnel. Occasionally they will dig into hanging plant baskets. Striated Pardalotes (left) either dig a tunnel or nest in tree knot-holes; those in Tasmania and the south, with striped crowns, are more likely to nest in trees, while northern birds with black crowns are much more likely to dig burrows. Southern birds are likely to nest in loose colonies while northern birds are more solitary while breeding. A heap of soil left in the garden will often inspire a pair to breed. It is hard to know what advantage there is in tunnel nesting, as many nests containing chicks are dug out by goannas. Two to five white eggs are laid. Chicks stay in the nest a week or more longer than similarly sized birds and appear to become independent quicker once they leave the nest.

Metallic Starling

Large numbers of Metallic Starlings migrate each year from New Guinea to north-eastern Queensland, from Cape York to about Sarina, arriving in August–September and leaving in April, although times may vary and some may stay throughout the year. Soon after arrival flocks begin building their large suspended woven nests in tight colonies; often the same trees are used year after year, commonly in towns. Much noisy squabbling and stealing of nest material occurs. Other birds like friarbirds, figbirds and orioles may also nest in the colonies. Young birds (inset) have the underparts white with black streaking. Grey Goshawks regularly visit colonies, even nesting in some.

Spangled Drongo

Superficially like the Metallic Starling, the Spangled Drongo is easily distinguished by its 'fish-tail'. It has a wider range in the north and east, from about Broome, Western Australia, to about Jervis Bay, New South Wales. In the east it is partly migratory and is unusual in having a reverse migration, with some heading south in winter. It feeds on insects often caught in the air, takes nectar, and occasionally captures small birds like Mistletoebirds in flight. It is quite noisy and given to mimicry, including calls of raptors. Drongos will visit gardens and accept hand-outs in the form of strips of meat. The nest is a hanging basket placed towards the end of a horizontal branch. Three to five blotched pinkish eggs are laid.

Finches

S mall seed-eating birds, finches are welcome additions to any garden, particularly those with plenty of shelter in the form of shrubbery and understory. Fine bird-seed will attract them to the feeding table and plantings of native grasses such as kangaroo grass also provide sustenance. They need to drink frequently so water in the garden will attract them. For much of the year finches travel in flocks, usually small in numbers, but the Chestnut-breasted Mannikin and some others gather in large flocks when conditions are favourable. In the breeding season the flocks break up into pairs, with some courting males holding grass stems in their beaks. Nests are quite bulky affairs, constructed from grass, rather like an untidy bottle on its side with an entrance at one end more or less concealed by wisps of grass. Some species like the Chestnut-breasted Mannikin build the nest in long grass, while the Red-browed, Star and Double-barred Finches choose shrubs and small trees. In the inland Zebra Finches favour the introduced prickly acacia, and in the north the Crimson Finch will often build under eaves as well as in pandanus, banana plants and palms. Often only the female builds but is usually accompanied by the male. Eggs are white and as many as eight may be laid, although 4–6 is the usual clutch. Both parents feed the chicks on seeds by regurgitation. Chicks have specific markings inside the mouth, and some species have small luminescent globes on the gape. Once they leave the nest chicks continue to be fed by the adults for a short time, then quickly learn to find their own food and join neighbouring flocks.

The Double-barred Finch ranges in the east and north from south-eastern New South Wales to about Broome, Western Australia; its range is slowly extending southward.

The Zebra Finch is an abundant bird of the inland wherever there is water and shelter, although they are able to survive without drinking for several months.

The Crimson Finch occupies northern Australia from the Fitzroy River, Western Australia, to mid-eastern Queensland. Like many finches its range is contracting. It is shown grasping grass seed-heads in its claws, a typical feeding pattern.

The Chestnut-breasted Mannikin is found in grasslands across northern and eastern Australia from about Derby, Western Australia, to the Shoalhaven River, New South Wales. In the north it has been known to interbreed with the Yellow-rumped Mannikin and to produce fertile hybrids, indicating a close relationship although they are very different in appearance.

The Red-browed Finch ranges in eastern Australia from Cape York, Queensland, to Kangaroo Island, South Australia. It is feral in Western Australia in the Darling Ranges and foothills east of Perth.

DISAPPEARING FINCHES

The ranges of a number of finch species are contracting. The Star Finch and Black-throated Finch were once found in New South Wales but now only occur much further north. Gouldian Finches now occupy a fraction of their former territory. Numbers of others like the Crimson Finch and Pictorella Finch are dwindling. What is to blame? Replacement of native grasses with introduced species is one probable cause, as well as burning off in grasslands at inappropriate times; the proliferation of cats is another; possibly diseases that came with introduced cagebirds are a cause.

Introduced Passerines

*I*n the 19th century many settlers from the Old Country were nostalgic for the birds and mammals they had left behind in England. To remedy what they saw as a lack of familiar creatures, acclimatisation societies were set up to import them into Australia, tragically unmindful of the beauties around them and blissfully ignorant of the damage some of the imports would cause. Each state had its own society with its own agenda. Rabbits, hares, foxes, deer and carp were released with devastating effect. Many species of birds from Europe and Asia were imported as well – most, thankfully, failed to survive, but those that did acclimatise, quickly flourished and spread. Among them are species that visit gardens, for example the House Sparrow, Tree Sparrow, European Goldfinch, European Greenfinch, Common Blackbird, Common Myna and Common Starling. Non-passerines that were introduced included Spotted and Laughing Turtle-Doves and gamebirds. The Laughing Kookaburra was introduced into Western Australia. Some birds that were kept in aviaries were not deliberately introduced but escaped in sufficient numbers to breed and expand their ranges, for example the Nutmeg Mannikin and Red-whiskered Bulbul. Some native birds that escaped from aviaries now occupy areas outside their natural ranges, including corellas, Rainbow Lorikeets and Red-browed Finches. They are basically ferals.

Top: Nutmeg Mannikin; Centre: Common Starling; Bottom: European Goldfinch.

Clockwise from top left: House Sparrow; Red-whiskered Bulbul; Common Blackbird; Common Myna.

WHO WAS RESPONSIBLE?

Of the state acclimatisation societies formed in the mid-19th century the most active was the Victorian society. The driving force behind its many introductions was its president Edward Wilson. Thousands of individual birds of many species were released by the 1870s.

Native Plants, Their Uses and Flowering/Fruiting Times

*I*f every garden was suitably planted, imagine what birds and other wildlife could be attracted to our suburbs and even cities.

Below is a small sample of some natives, their uses and flowering/fruiting times

TREES

Acacia sp.	Wattles	ins, prolific s pods/seed	
" *dealbata*	Silver Wattle	ins, s pods, seed	Jun–Aug
Archontophoenix cunninghamiana	Bangalow Palm	fru	Mar–May
Banksia serrata	Old Man Banksia	nect, ins, fru	Jan–Apr
Callistemon viminalis	Weeping Bottlebrush	nect, ins, shel	Oct–Jan
Callitris rhomboidea	Port Jackson Pine	fru, ins, nest	
Castanospermum australe	Black Bean	nect, shel	Oct–Jan
Elaeocarpus reticulatus	Blueberry Ash	fru	Mar–Jul
Eucalyptus sp.	Eucalypts	nect, ins, fruit, seed, sap, shel, nest, hol	
Ficus coronata	Sandpaper Fig	fru, seed	Dec–Apr
Grevillea robusta	Silky Oak	nect, ins, seed	Oct–Dec
Melaleuca sp.	Paperbarks, Tea trees	nect, ins	
" *styphelioides*	Prickly Paperbark	nect, ins, shel, nest	Dec–Jan
Melicope elleryana	Pink Euodia	nect, seed	Nov–Jan
" *rubra*	Little Evodia	nect, fru, seed	

SHRUBS

Acacia sp.	Wattles	ins, prolific s pods/seed	
" *armata*	Kangaroo thorn	pric, den, shel, nest, har	Aug–Oct
" *suaveolens*	Sweet Wattle	s pods/seed	Mar–Jun
Baeckea sp.		shel, ins, nest	
Banksia sp.	Banksias	nect, ins, shel	
" *ericifolia*	Heath-leafed Banksia	nec, ins	Apr–Aug
" *heliantha*	Oak-leaved Dryandra	ins, fru, nest	
" *spinulosa*	Hairpin Banksia	nec, ins, long flowering	Mar–Oct
Bursaria spinosa	Blackthorn	nect, ins, nest, shel	Nov–Jan
Callistemon sp.	Bottlebrushes	nect, ins, seed, shel	
" *macropunctatus*	Scarlet Bottlebrush	nect, ins, seed	Oct–Jan
Correa sp.	Correa	nect, seed	
" *reflexa*	Native Fuchsia	nect, ins, ber	May–Nov
Eremophila maculata	Spotted Emu Bush	nect	May–Nov
Grevillea sp.	Grevillea	nect, ins, fru	
" *banksii*	Banks' Grevillea	nect, ins	all year
" *cultivar*	Robynn Gordan	pric, nect, nest, shel	all year
" *juniperina*	Prickly spider flower	pric, shel, nest	Aug–Nov
Hakea sp.	Needle bushes	shel, nect, nest	
" *petiolaris*	Sea-urchin hakea	nest, shel,	May–Jun
" *propinqua*	Blacknose	shel, nest, seed	Jun–Oct
" *sericea*	Silky Hakea	ins, fru, shel, nest/material	May–Oct
Leptospermum sp.	Tea trees	ins, shel, nest	
Melaleuca sp.	Honey myrtles		
" *hypericifolia*	Hillock bush	nect, den, har	Sep–Jan
" *lateritia*	Robin Red-breast	nect, har	Dec–May

Solanum aviculare	Kangaroo Apple	fru	Sep–Dec
Westringia fruticosa	Coast rosemary	shel, nest	

GROUND COVERS
prostrate forms of above

Anigozanthos sp.	Kangaroo paws	nect	Sep–Dec
Lomandra sp.	Mattrush	shel	
Poa labillardieri	Tussock grass	seeds, shel, nest material	
Stipa sp.	Spear grasses	seeds, nest material	
Themeda triandra	Kangaroo grass	seeds, shel, nest material	Sep–Jan

OTHERS

Doryanthes excelsa	Gymea lily	nect, ins	Sep–Dec
Xanthorrhoea sp.	Grass trees	nect, ins, seeds, shel, nest	Sep–Oct

nect – nectar; ins – insect; s pods – seed pods; fru – fruit; shel – shelter; roo – roost; pric – prickly; har – hardy; hol – hollows; den – dense; ber – berries.

To deter cats try planting *Coleus canina*, lavender, geranium or lemon thyme near water and seed; cats supposedly hate the smell of these plants.

Lethal predators!

After habitat loss, cats are the biggest threat to our birds – an efficient, very agile hunter, with both teeth and claws as their weapons. Dogs are a little less dangerous, particularly if trained. Though pet owners think their cat is too well fed or lazy to attack wildlife, their predatory instincts are too strong – they can't help themselves, so owners need to give the birds a chance. A simple but not fool-proof idea is to attach a bell to the pet's collar, giving birds that hear it an opportunity to escape. The best solution is to create an outdoor area, completely enclosed in mesh and attached to the house next to a window or pet door, so the pet has access to fresh air and sun but can't play havoc with the birds.

CAT FOOD?

Assuming there are a million pet cats in Australia, and each kills one bird a month, that is 12 million birds a year, a very conservative estimate for backyard slaughter!

INDEX